Frontiers of the Caribbean

MANCHESTER
1824

Manchester University Press

THEORY FOR A GLOBAL AGE

Series Editor: Gurminder K. Bhambra

Globalisation is widely viewed as a current condition of the world, but there is little engagement with how this changes the way we understand it. The Theory for a Global Age series addresses the impact of globalisation on the social sciences and humanities. Each title will focus on a particular theoretical issue or topic of empirical controversy and debate, addressing theory in a more global and interconnected manner. With contributions from scholars across the globe, the series will explore different perspectives to examine globalisation from a global viewpoint. True to its global character, the Theory for a Global Age series will be available for online access worldwide via Creative Commons licensing, aiming to stimulate wide debate within academia and beyond.

To Juke
Best wishes
Philip (xx)

Frontiers of the Caribbean

Philip Nanton

Manchester University Press

Published by Manchester University Press
Altrincham Street, Manchester M1 7JA
www.manchesteruniversitypress.co.uk

British Library Cataloguing-in-Publication Data
A catalogue record for this book is available from the British Library

Library of Congress Cataloging-in-Publication Data applied for

ISBN 978 1526 11374 0 hardback
ISBN 978 1526 11373 3 paperback
ISBN 978 1526 11492 1 open access

First published 2017

Typeset by Out of House Publishing
Printed by Lightning Source

For Jane,
Ashley,
Roxanne,
Corin
and Tumi

Contents

Series editor's introduction

The Theory for a Global Age series seeks to shift the perspective from which we view the world when we consider its global condition. Given that the majority of scholarly work on the global locates its centre within the ambit of Europe and North America, then, of necessity, the rest of the world appears simply as residue, as periphery. In contrast, this series seeks to highlight the work of authors who make central what is regarded otherwise as marginal and, from that re-centring, aims to rethink mainstream understandings of the global. This is the intention and outcome of Philip Nanton's extraordinary book, *Frontiers of the Caribbean*.

Nanton uses the nuance and force specific to creative expression to present to us a social and sociological analysis of Caribbean societies, in particular St Vincent and the Grenadines. He moves effortlessly from rich, evocative descriptions of the natural cartography of the island to the complex social geographies exemplified by a variety of instances of fellowship, camaraderie and hierarchy that distinguish life on and between islands. From the rituals around the felling of a gommier tree, described in Mike Kirkwood's foreword, to the social dynamics of the marketplace – 'They display ... their small-scale items for sale: heaps of fruit, ground provisions, braziers, sports trainers, telephone cards and boot-legged DVDs and CDs. A few self-styled preachers with clanging bell, Bible, tambourine or squeaking microphone stand at intersections and shout warnings of hell fire or extol the benefits of repentance' – Nanton vividly depicts the universal rhythms of life in their specificity on a small island.

The idea of the frontier, which is a key motif of the book, is not simply used to delimit what is contained within it, but provides multiple opportunities for discussion of the productive openings created through its crossings and transgressions. The island itself is located as a frontier, and as the contested place of internal frontiers, specifically between civilisation and wilderness: both produced by and productive of the global forces that shaped the modern world and continue to do so. Nanton points to the way in which general discussions of civilisation, while implicitly counter-posed to wilderness, rarely address wilderness as a constitutive correlate to it. This imbalance is addressed in *Frontiers of the Caribbean* through careful attention to the history and contemporary presence of the wilderness within forms of Caribbean modernity. The wilderness is that which refuses domestication, that refuses completion, and that evades policing. It is a social landscape, as much as it is a natural one, and it is given form also through Nanton's discussion of the 'Wilderness People', spiritual Baptists who, through their transgression of standard practices, created new forms of community across and beyond the frontiers of established religion.

Frontiers of the Caribbean draws on sources not usually regarded as central to the social science literature, but the eclecticism of method brings together new connections and interconnections that burst through existing lines of enquiry. The making and remaking of the Caribbean is a story of the creation and recreation of boundaries and of bonds – bonds of domination and of solidarity. It is a story that has to be represented and imagined – to capture the nature of the past and the possibilities for the future. Nanton's book satisfies our need for both knowledge and imaginative connection.

Gurminder K. Bhambra
University of Warwick

Foreword: the roaring

You can't get away from it: the roaring, I mean. On our celebrity-haunted Grenadines (Mustique, Bequia, Canouan …) it will subside to the merest susurration of sea breezes, of parrot fish nibbling at coral, of fine grains of coral-white sand in the tilt of wavelets. But come nightfall it will be back with the squeaking of bats, the keening of mosquitoes, and the surround-sound shrilling of cricket and cicada. And under these, but also in these, in a concatenated mesh as fine as your mosquito netting, after the last small plane has landed and the last ferry docked, you will hear the roaring, the very breathing of our mainland.

Our small island is a volcanic beast, roaring from its lair 4,000 feet above the (mainly mineral-black or -grey) beaches of the Atlantic on our windward side and the Caribbean Sea to leeward. A hundred miles down is the inferno. Tectonic plates meet in a classic pressure arc. Think of the crease that results when you press your thumb down on the surface of a ping-pong ball, then trace the arc of the Antilles. The Atlantic plate, new-minted along the mid-ocean ridge and pushing westwards at the rate of a few centimetres a year, meets the Caribbean plate along that arc, and tucks under it, deflecting down towards the mantle. Our inferno is one of the hotspots where this process creates a magma spiral and an active volcano visible as an island for about a million years.

The seawater sucked down in the subduction has been shown to issue from the mouth of the beast in gouts of steam; it is an element in our aquifers, another note in the constant under-song of the countless folded ravines we call 'gutters'. We are suffused with energies we cannot dispel, with an almost intolerable richness in our new-made soil. Two-hundred-and-fifty years ago we grew the tobacco that, exported to Macuba in Martinique by our 'Black Caribs' (Garinagu, or Garifuna, as they still prefer to be known), ended up in the 'maccaboy' stuffed into the most prestigious snuffboxes that circulated in Jonathan's Coffeehouse in Change Alley, the avatar of the London Stock Exchange.

Along with the first lists of stock and commodity prices, coffeehouse patrons took in the grand plan of Newton's universe through artfully constructed 'orreries', displayed newly invented technologies, hatched colonising companies and new wars of domination, and wrote verse and prose that celebrated or satirised all these trappings of capitalism's emergence. These days, Amsterdam's coffeehouses are a good place to reflect on how it all began and how it is ending … and if you choose to enhance the reverie with the most expensive marijuana you can buy, chances are you will end up smoking a substance grown in exactly the same soil (DeVolet, on our forested north-western coast) that afforded Europe its first heady sniff of the future all those years ago.

Perhaps we are fated to supply no more than the intoxicating plume of consciousness that is exhaled by and lingers over the tumultuous creations of modernity. Perhaps this role will continue to occlude the reality that we have been deeply implicated, from the first eruptions and since, in the making of this brave new world (first named for places like us) of which we continue to be an inescapable part, even as we are remodelled into a white-sand (tankered in) holiday destination (though once we served as a laboratory for the financial calculations and industrial organisation of labour that shaped world production in the nineteenth and twentieth centuries). Meanwhile, we continue to remodel ourselves and each other.

Nicotiana tabacum and *Cannabis sativa* were brought or wandered here. Bligh finally planted his breadfruit in our once celebrated but now sadly petrified Botanical Gardens, among the first in our hemisphere. Breadfruit (*Artocarpus altilis*), in all its cultivars, and its near relative the jackfruit (*Artocarpus heterophyllus*), are famous for their genetic diversity, based on extremely rapid, prolific and repeated hybridisation. After two centuries as runaways in our mountains, under closer study our breadfruit may reveal some interesting mutations. Certainly, scientists have come here to study indigenous plants, birds and bats that are of interest precisely because they are still evolving. Everything that grows or breathes on our island (and even the restless boulders that tumble and clash in our torrential rivers) is continuously pushing up against, winding round, entangling and interfering with, burrowing under, or flowing over everything else. Our 'built environment' is so much a party to this relentless, continuous energy exchange – affording, adapting, merging, diverging – that it is almost impossible to tell our ruins from our unfinished projects.

That is why we roar. Even when our volcano is stilled (it last erupted on Good Friday 1979, to mark a controversial independence); even when the hurricanes give us a miss (we were overdue when Tomas found us out); even when the latest rainsquall has left the mountains – visible and audible from afar, deafening on a tin roof, then dissolving into thin air before reaching the coast – the roaring continues, taken up by toad, beetle and bat, by bird and beast, and amplified exponentially by our human habitudes. If our June carnival is the annual climax, it has been building throughout the year, with minor crescendos at Christmas and Easter, and a daily hubbub that starts with the mobile fish hawker's insistent conch trumpet and ends with the ice-cream van's relentless circling of the Mulberry Bush in search of a Muffin Man last seen when London Bridge was Falling Down.

Nightfall brings no relief. We have more dogs than people. We have cockerels that sense the new day just after midnight and donkeys that people the island with lewd and lusty nightmares. But when the fireflies are out something extraordinary may happen. The Cuban writer Antonio Benítez-Rojo invokes a certain Caribbean way of walking, in which:

> a person might feel that he wants to walk not with his feet alone, and to this end he imbues the muscles of his neck, back, abdomen, arms, in short all his muscles, with their own rhythm, different from the rhythm of footsteps, which no longer dominate … What has happened is that the centre of the rhythmic ensemble framed by the footsteps has been displaced and now it runs from muscle to muscle, stopping here and there and illuminating in intermittent succession, *like a firefly*, each rhythmic focus of the body. (Benítez-Rojo, 1996: 19)

Sometimes – you have to listen for it, but once heard it is as inescapable as a dream you long to dream again – our polyrhythm prospers and the noises we are so full of segue into sounds and sweet airs that give delight and hurt not, even if a thousand twangling instruments hum about our ears.

Every weekday morning we take our roaring to the round island road: a lasso woven from tar, concrete and *terra firma* that snakes along our leeward and windward coastlines from the noose-knot of Kingstown, our capital. We are in bondage to this road, ever more reliant on the capital for jobs and imported goods, including the staple foods we used to grow. The road is narrow as a ligature, and our lives chafe at its edges. It twists and ascends sharply, turns and descends; its coils tighten interminably. The body of our island is asymmetrically ribbed, with multiform ridges that diverge from a central, rainforested spine that tends southeast–northwest, separating our windward and leeward coasts. Three towering 'volcanic centres' – two ancient and dormant, the third the present roarer – define the discontinuous series of mountains that make up this backbone, at once a landscape and the island's autobiography, its physical signature. A journey along the high ridges, from the south-east to the present site of the volcano on Mount Soufriere in the north-west, would recapitulate the main events of the island's geological and ecostructural making, the way of the volcano. At our north-western corner the road falters and is incomplete; the spinning lasso is out of its range and loses form; passing overhead, a light plane may report disturbances; in this sector our soils are richest and our future indeterminable.

It is this body – with the ways it once taught us to move around its 'odd angles' and 'every fertile inch', learning infinite 'subtleties of the isle that will not let us believe things certain' – that the road now holds captive. Along the shackled flanks of ridges we now build our homes tight to the roadside and hold them precariously in place with high concrete-block retaining walls and steep cemented access points. The road has no pavements; typically it is edged by a deep concrete drain abutting the high ground to which the houses cling, and a precipitous drop on the other side of a crumbling margin of waste ground. Along these margins pedestrians – including tiny school children, the old and frail, and those who bellow and threaten to hurl themselves at passing cars – move at considerable risk to their lives. There be monsters, including concrete mixers. For some reason these vehicles are driven at high speed. To encounter three of them racing to a new construction site in convoy is a definitively stomach-churning experience. Lazier, but genuinely juggernautical on such a road as ours, are the increasingly common container lorries. Equipped with hooters as deafening as fog-horns, they bellow mournfully within our maze of blind corners, forcing other vehicles to halt as they shudder past. Frequently enough, the combination of a hairpin bend and a forty-five-degree gradient is too much for them, despite the audacious skill of their drivers. Capsizing, they wait several days to be rescued, as helpless as upturned beetles. Overburdened by these behemoths and an exponential rise in the number of private vehicles (often imported second-hand from Japan), and undermined by torrential rain for nine months of the year, our road is constantly shedding its wrinkled and peeling skin, and coming out in a fresh rash of potholes.

Our lives are lived under the spell of this road, a smear of belched-up tar from the innards of a restless earth. All the enforced journeys of our lives are made on its scabby dragon's back, and most of our enchanted wanderings too. But it is also our stage, and across it we roar under its roaring, and seek out the faces we know, and shout the names of friend and foe. Valley still calls to valley, though now all the valleys are plaited into the same rope. Recently I made a journey along it with an old man whose early life – he had been a woodcutter – had been lived peripatetically on the ridge lines that conjoin valley and valley, windward and leeward. As we counted the number of hairpin bends in the road – more than fifty in the course of our half-hour journey – he remarked that there had once been many more. The older road snared every descending ridge, snaking in and out to reveal small settlements that the road now bypasses. All these folds within folds he had known as intimately as the wrinkles on his mother's face. He had known what it is to leave one place as a venturer beyond the familiar – therefore a potential outcast and ne'er-do-well – and to enter another as a sinister stranger who might simultaneously be a bearer of the new and the useful.

A special place in his memory of how we were – perhaps its fount – is held by an event that links this ridge-walking style of communication with another just as old. He tells of felling gommier trees (*Dacryodes hexandra*), the giant gumtrees that signpost the way of the volcano through the rainforest. For this task the woodcutters would assemble a small army of mountain-goers – men and women, young and old – and lead them up from the villages below. This rite of passage – a once-in-a-lifetime event for many of the participants – is a reminder that, although the ridge-walkers were outcasts/strangers in the eyes of their more sedentary kin and neighbours, they nevertheless held to a way of life that was bred in the bone. When we 'shout' each other in public places – in joyous recognition, in open challenge, in feigned remonstrance or even in abusive imprecation – we are using a communicative form that was bred in the mountains, in a zone of freedom, discovery, danger and suspicion – and within a form of fellowship in which all these states of mind were woven together. The journey to the height and the heart of the island, where the gommier trees grow, was a celebration of that fellowship.

The felling of a gommier tree was followed by an arduous portage down through the forest to the coast that took several days. While the work would consume all the energy of the assembled villagers, the ardour of the enterprise was replenished at the end of each stage by feasting, singing and storytelling around their campfires, intermittently visible from below, deep into the night. In this way the rhythmic ensemble of focused bodies would be transferred to the gommier, teaching the giant tree to walk. For its part, the gommier would light the fires that marked the stages of its progress towards the sea. When mountain-goers come upon a gommier tree in the forest they scarify its bark, allowing its resin to ooze out, forming bulbous weals. These are plucked from the tree by the next traveller and compacted into balls ('gummy'), which form a portable source of fire. Making a campfire on the wet forest floor is a delicate matter. Gummy not only makes the fire thrive but also releases an aroma that wafts as randomly as a priest shakes his censer.

Gommiers began crossing seas almost as soon as they learned to walk down the mountain from the high forests. From the sixteenth century, canoes or pirogues (both words are of Carib origin) transported African slaves captured from Spanish colonies deep in the Gulf of Mexico back to our 'capital of the Carib republic'. Captured or liberated? In the Island Carib language the word for 'slave' also meant 'son-in-law'. And the ethno-genesis of the Garifuna began with these early additions to our population (more African people landed from wrecked slave ships, and there was a steady influx of 'runaway negroes' from nearby Barbados in the century between the first sugar plantations there and the colonisation of St Vincent by the British in 1763). Before and after colonisation, despite an embargo enforced by British warships, Garifuna pirogues took their tobacco and other contraband products to Macuba and other destinations. In later colonial times these craft continued to be our main communicative device before the road was built. Within living memory the leeward side of our island was connected to Kingstown by a fleet of thirty-foot, multi-oared giant canoes ('canoe-boats' as they had come to be called) that operated a regular service ferrying passengers, produce and animals to the capital. Each major settlement had its own champion and there was great rivalry between the crews. The gommiers that walked down the mountain would be hollowed out and fashioned with axe, adze and fires that fed on their own resinous hearts.

But before the road, or any roads, the gommier boats linked the various nodes of life on the island on its windward and leeward shores. As simultaneously and expeditiously, they linked St Vincent not only to its Grenadines, but also to the other archipelagos of which it formed a part – to the arc of the eastern Antilles and beyond. Crossing ridges or seas we are in the thrall of a dynamic that moves us from deeply insular habitations – whether bounded by mountains or shorelines – to the multiple thresholds of other valleys or islands. In the 'first time' of the Garifuna these encompassed the entire Caribbean region, and they have since been extended by emigration to niches within New York, Greater London and beyond. Interestingly, the Garifuna Diaspora has both foretold and shadowed the late- and postcolonial movement of what has become the Vincentian nation.

Deported from the island after two wars of conquest (the second of which at the end of the eighteenth century intersected with the French-Haitian revolutionary ferment, which provided the Garifuna with important allies and comrades-in-arms), they were first dumped on Balliceaux, a 'bare, hard rock' in the vicinity of the mainland where 5,000 people over nine months experienced what would now be termed a genocidal episode. Half the number survived what may have been a typhus epidemic (drinking water was in short supply) and were then moved to the island of Roatan off the coast of Honduras. Generation by generation, the Garifuna have reconstituted and remembered them-selves as a people in Honduras, Belize, Guatemala and Nicaragua. Like Vincentians, they have a diasporic presence beyond these coun-tries that exceeds numerically their 'home' populations. Their cultural renaissance – most popularly expressed in Punta Rock, a musical genre derived from performances first enjoyed on St Vincent two or three centuries ago – made them known to other diasporic groups compara-tively recently, a process hastened by internet sites and blogs. Estimates of present Garifuna and Vincentian world populations both hover around the quarter-of-a-million mark. In places like Brooklyn and the Bronx, *Doppelgänger* Vincentian and Garifuna elements may have rubbed shoulders unknowingly, the latter preserving a language, music and culture expressive of a precolonial island where the former first became aware of themselves in colonial or postcolonial times. Most Vincentians in the diaspora dream of returning, and many do. Return to the native place is also a feature of the *dugu*, a Garifuna funerary rite that brings together community members from the diaspora, extended families and ancestor spirits (the *gubida*). Balliceaux has in recent times become the object of an annual Garifuna pilgrimage, and attempts by St Vincent's current administration to set up exclusive tourist develop-ment on the islet have been opposed on the grounds of its importance as a national heritage site and a nesting ground for seabirds. In the trad-itional enactment of the rite, the pirogues are out all night, returning at dawn with the *gubida* to a shoreline decked out in palm fronds where the *buyia* (shaman) and the populace are waiting. It is many years since a sea-leaning gommier was felled on our mountains, but I know at least one old woodcutter who has kept his two-handed saw in working order, the blade encased in its bamboo scabbard for easy travel to the high ridges where the *gubida* grew their maccaboy tobacco.

These days nearly all mountain haunters who reach as far as the ridge lines and rainforest regions are growing ganja, a plant domesticated on St Vincent as recently as the 1970s. But the threshold between small mountain farmers and ganja crews is subtle and indistinct, whether we conceive it topographically or socially. The highest provision grounds reach deep into the secondary forest that fringes the rainforest zone. And ganja growers are nearly all from farming families. Many have switched by degrees from food crops, weighing the dangers and rewards through a calculus whose variables include global and local markets, age, family responsibilities, and employment opportunities. The Rastafarianism that many espouse is only the latest in a series of diverse, often syncretic religious and cultural expressions that are evolving along with so much else on an island where 'demonic cults' ('Shakers' in the late nineteenth century) may turn into staid patriarchal religions within a generation (the Shakers are now the Spiritual Baptist Church; already a similar trend within Rastafarianism can be observed).

Ganja growers are no different from most Vincentians in relying on a survival strategy that is as asymmetric and multiform as the island itself. The same individual may be a government employee, pursue a trade, run an agency for imported items, have a vehicle or machinery for hire – and, all the while, be a registered farmer whose main sideline is ganja. In short, we are roarers because we are hustlers. And the default métier of the Vincentian hustler is undoubtedly the passenger van, usually a refurbished import of Japanese manufacture, often fitted, upholstered and spray-painted on the island, and capable of carrying eighteen passengers (with ingenious flip-down seating in the companion-way for the last to board). Their sound systems churn out music suited to the route – reggae classics on the deep leeward run, dancehall music for the run from the capital to the tourist enclaves of the near windward coast. Although the vans and their drivers are demonised by the self-driving middle class – as noisy, inconsiderate, a law unto themselves, conduits for drugs and lower-depth chicanery in all forms – the vans can and do claim (there is an active van owners' association) to be a self-seeded, self-organising public transport system. It is one of the few public services on our island that really does work – fares are low, journeys are rapid, waiting times are brief and passenger security on the whole is excellent.

The life of a van – like many of the themes sketched in what I have written here – is a topic in itself. Suffice it to say that visitors who wish to claim, returning home, that they know what we are like, would be well advised to see the island from, and most certainly from within, these ubiquitous microcosms that hurtle through our collective life. It is something of an honour to be offered a seat (with seatbelt!) up front with the driver; his 'sweetie' usually occupies the place between you and him. Once you have adjusted to the uncompromising speed of his driving, you will have a grand view of our roadside and further vistas, sea and mountain, and mountain beyond mountain. You will also begin to appreciate the considerable skill with which he drives, and his extensive and lightning-fast rapport with other (oncoming) van drivers, particularly over the protocols and intuitions governing pothole negotiation on bends and narrow stretches. A local story tells of a rare falling-out between drivers, one of whom was a well-known road warrior, a big-belly, bellicose man with a fierce and disconcerting squint. Forced to brake hard, he leaned out of his window to reprimand a driver who had failed to read his intentions: 'Why you cyan' look where you goin'?'. But his adversary won the bout hands down (on his horn as he retreated) with: 'Why you cyan' go where you lookin'!'

Once you have your bearings, the place to be is in the innards of the van. The views may be more fleeting, but you are better placed to savour a passage through the roaring bloodstream of our daily life, often quite as theatrical a place as, say, James I's Whitehall Palace on Hallowmas night (1 November) 1611, when Shakespeare's *The Tempest* was first acted by the King's Men. With a full complement of passengers, body cleaving to body through those fifty hairpin bends, the throb of the music answering the pulse of the engine, people are literally thrown together, and a strong sense emerges of the 'ahl we' Vincentians claim to be. The Ariel of this island within an island is undoubtedly the conductor, and he does his spriting gently enough. Very occasionally a woman takes the part, but usually he is a young man, elegantly shirted and coiffeured. If never quite invisible, he is an agile shape-changer. Appearing from nowhere as you approach the central bus station in town, he will take charge of your parcels and escort you to the van. Effectively you are his prisoner, but his spell is effective, too, and you follow willingly enough where he leads. As, stop by stop, the van fills, he adjusts his lithe body to the available interior space, until finally he seems to hover over his charges, simultaneously sliding the door closed without damaging his wings. With several of the passengers he appears to be on intimate terms, though the prettier girls may pout their denials, suck their teeth and refuse to meet his gaze. He stows sacks of provisions and buckets of fish miraculously here and there, and then hands them out to waiting vendors at places where the driver pulls in without ever quite stopping.

At a certain time of day, when the crèches close, he becomes the pied piper of a troop of toddlers, leading them from roadside establishment to the waiting van and bestowing them expertly in such passenger niches as remain – they usually end up in the row immediately behind the driver and adjacent to his own seat (or hovering zone) at the door – or else releasing them into the arms of passengers known to the children. At stops along the way each of his charges is swiftly and safely delivered to a family member who is waiting to receive the child.

In addition to their value as a public service – and in such matters as the intimate and safe transfer of small children between crèche and home, or the therapeutic reassessment of identity in an impromptu, pell-mell dialogue, they endow 'public' with a higher order of meaning than such services can claim to offer in more 'developed' countries – vans represent a significant entry point into the 'lived' (and thus 'real') economy of the one-third of national income estimated to derive from the production and sale of marijuana. Frequently enough, the owner-driver of a van has purchased his vehicle and established his business with 'investment capital' accumulated via his ganja cultivation. His conductor and co-drivers may also be crew members in his ganja 'farm'.

In this and other ways the mountains and the ridge systems descending from them are sutured to the road along which homes are precipitously stacked, and by which lives are bound under steadily increasing pressure. Hurricanes hit us or miss us and take their roaring elsewhere. Behind us or before us, under us or above us, all around us and most of all within us, the volcano persists. At full moon, as in our old-time ring dances, we gaze at the unattainable object of desire, at a remnant of the earth's formative crust that still regulates our seas, our bodies, our growing seasons and our dreams. And continue to make ourselves out of 'such stuff as dreams are made on', our Ur rock endlessly cycled and transformed by constant, eruptive shudders of energy expelled by 'the inexorable vice of tectonic plates'. We roar.

Punctuation Marks

Where sea and land meet, begin there.
The ampersand, the join, is a fault
that caused jagged peaks to rise
from the ocean's floor
spanning a vacant gulf.
On any map of the world they are footnotes
reminders of nature's force.

Long ago, nomads, fragile as their pottery
skimming waves, trekking from south to north
stopped once too often for wood and water
and perished.
From the pre-ceramic Cibony
to the ceramics of Saladoid and Suazoid
we know them by their shards.
Common island Caribs
sunk in a murderous tide
that flowed from East to West
bearing assassins and poets
discoverers of the new world.

Come nearer, focus on one dot of an island.
I was born there, on the rim of a volcano
on the edge of a large full stop
where the sand is black
where the hills are a gun-barrel blue
where the sea perpetually dashes at the shoreline
trying to reclaim it all.

    Philip Nanton (first published as 'I' (Nanton,
                          1992))

Acknowledgements

Some years ago, in a plush, official government palace in Bridgetown, Barbados called the Frank Collymore Hall, I had a chance meeting with Kamau Brathwaite, Barbados's legendary poet and historian. After some polite shadow-boxing and possibly a slippery remark or two from me he came to the point. He posed me a seemingly direct and simple question. 'And what', he asked, 'does Philip Nanton have to say about the Caribbean?'. His challenge has haunted me for ten years or more and I suppose that this text is one response to his question. My struggle to answer his question in the way that I have chosen in this book has led me to incur many debts that I would like to acknowledge.

In the early stages of thinking about and writing this book it was my good fortune to be befriended by Vincentian-born Mike Kirkwood, who also has roots in South Africa. I owe him much for his enthusiasm about things Vincentian: our many discussions around the idea of the frontier in the Caribbean and elsewhere, and not least his willingness to allow his essay 'The Roaring' to introduce my text. The genial Father Mark DaSilva, who served his Grenadines parish for some fifteen years, knows more about the flora, fauna and people of that region than anyone I know. He encouraged me to write about the Grenadines and I took up his suggestion in my own way. Others from St Vincent, including Adrian Fraser, Vonnie Roudette, Caroline Sardine, William Abbott and Deborah Dalrymple, have offered kindness, support and encouragement at various stages of the thinking and writing process.

In Barbados, Woodville Marshall, Cleve Scott and Nan Peacocke each made time to read early drafts of the text, and each offered encouragement and criticism. Avinash Persaud, with a quiet patience, introduced me to some of the finer points of the financial services world. Christine Barrow read a later draft and helpfully suggested, in particular, that a perspective on religion in St Vincent would not go amiss, and she was right. Jane Bryce read every draft and offered lots of constructive criticism.

I have held many helpful email discussions about the Caribbean, small island states and the frontier with Shalini Puri, who lives and teaches in the USA.

In the last century, when I lived in England, it was again my good luck to be a student of and get to know as a friend the cheerful and supportive Robin Cohen. His enthusiastic response to a draft of a few chapters of this work gave added encouragement that perhaps I had something to say. Caroline Wintersgill, now at Manchester University Press, freed me to say whatever that something was in my own way. The unfailingly responsive and encouraging Gurminder Bhambra, editor of Theory for a Global Age, has allowed me to say it as part of that series. Three unidentified readers said some kind things and made telling comments about the draft manuscript. I have tried to be as enthusiastic in my response to them as they were in their criticism. I had many early discussions about writing this book with Marian Fitzgerald.

Jane Bryce, my partner, kicked my arse (metaphorically) and told me – many times – to get on with it before the curtains close. She was, as in many things, so right.

That, I suppose, is the gist of my debts of gratitude and how what appears in the pages below got done. But for what has been done I, and I alone, must say: *mea culpa, mea maxima culpa.*

Every effort has been made to obtain permission to contact the copyright holders of 'Shaker Funeral', and the publisher will be pleased to be informed of any errors and omissions for correction in future editions.

Abbreviations

CARICOM	Caribbean Community
CRD	Canouan Resorts Development Ltd
GDP	gross domestic product
OECD	Organisation for Economic Co-Operation and Development
SVG	St Vincent and the Grenadines
TCMP	Tobago Cays Marine Park
UN	United Nations
UNDP	United Nations Development Programme
UNODC	United Nations Office on Drugs and Crime

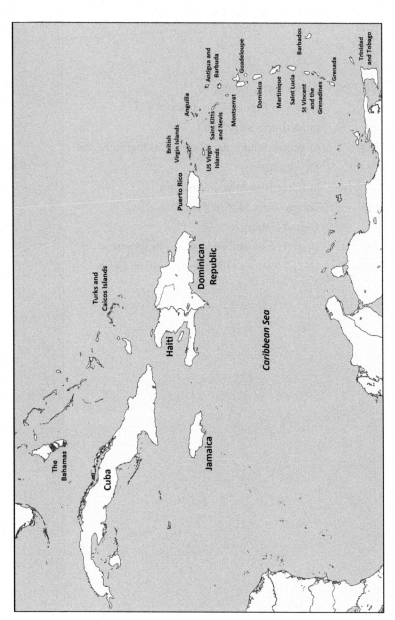

Map 1 The Caribbean (adapted from Shadowxfox / Wikimedia Commons / CC BY SA 3.0)

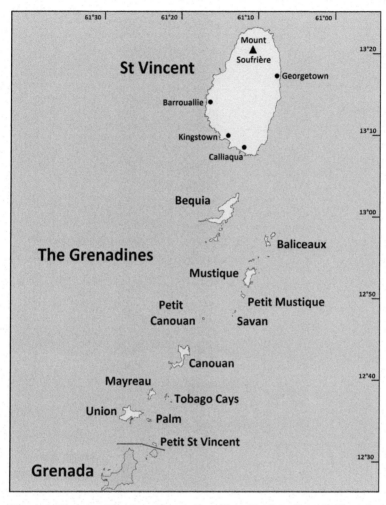

Map 2 St Vincent and the Grenadines (adapted from NordNordWest / Wikimedia Commons / CC BY SA 2.0)

Introduction

This book represents a synthesis of three distinct tendencies or directions that my academic and creative work has taken. One is an awareness of the need for reimagining the Caribbean in a world context. This concern can be summarised in the question: how can a small, increasingly ignored, dependent region contribute to the dominant debate of the late twentieth and twenty-first centuries – i.e. the impact and meaning of globalisation? This question, it seems to me, comes even more clearly into focus when the perspective shifts from the relatively better known and more visible anglophone island states of Jamaica or Trinidad and Tobago, to an even more peripheral multi-island Caribbean microstate, St Vincent and the Grenadines (SVG). Can a country of some 389 km² (150 mi²) and a population of 109,462 (United Nations (UN) estimate for 2015) have much to say to the wider world beyond offering anti-colonial rhetoric, couched in a smattering of Marxist analysis and mixed with gratitude for occasional national or international handouts during natural disasters?

A second tendency of my work arises from an encounter with colonial and postcolonial conditions, both in the Caribbean and in Britain. At the intellectual level, I have become preoccupied by a number of issues, explored here, that colonial and postcolonial studies have ignored or find difficulty in including in their grander analyses. A commonplace of postcolonial studies is the supposed subversiveness of the colonial/postcolonial subject, through the tropes of mimicry, cultural hybridity, and writing or speaking back to the centre. Though these paradigms are useful, I have long felt uneasy at their failure to account for disjunctures and contradictions that play themselves out, I would suggest, in a context of local differences that have little to do with the metropolitan centre. An example I examine in this book is the history of the Shakers, or Spiritual Baptists, a religious practice with its roots in the St Vincent countryside that spread, first, to St Vincent's urban areas, and then to neighbouring islands, including Grenada, and Trinidad and Tobago. Since the nineteenth century, the community has differentiated itself from the Methodists – the church that, relative to the more mainstream Anglican and Roman Catholic churches, welcomed black social outcasts – by the prominent position it accords to women leaders. The challenge thus posed by the Shakers – essentially faith-based and located among the local black and rural labour force – is difficult to contain within the paradigms of mimicry, hybridity and speaking back to the centre. I would prefer to see it as creating a space for difference on the terrain of what postcolonial studies refers to as 'the periphery', but that, to those who live there, is far from peripheral. The tendency of postcolonial theory to recuperate every such local difference as a subversive act of 'speaking back' to the metropole obscures the autochthonous nature of a movement like the Spiritual Baptists, engendered out of specific local circumstances to which outside influence is itself marginal.

Furthermore, the smallness of the society I examine encourages an interactive analysis, between micro-level analysis (i.e. individuals) and the collective, in the form of both positive and negative developments in the public sphere. For example, I examine the role played by a self-educated ganja middle-man, sometime farmer and now urban café owner, who, by lobbying for the relaxation of the drug laws, intercedes between marijuana farmers and respectable mainstream society – the so-called 'good and great', both local and international. Among the former, of course, is the islands' inimitable Prime Minister, informally known throughout the Caribbean as 'Comrade Ralph', a charismatic leader whose closest associates have been socialist icons like Hugo Chavez and Fidel Castro, but whose best efforts have not prevailed in making socialism take root in Vincentian society. In this regard, the ganja warrior is closer to the spirit of the place than the political ideologue.

The third tendency explored in this book reflects a personal journey, away from conventional disciplinary analysis, primarily sociological, to the use of creative expression for social analysis in the context of the Caribbean. In a previous book, *Island Voices from St Christopher and the Barracudas* (Nanton, 2014a), I draw on my social observation of various Caribbean societies to dramatise and satirise a range of class, race and gender anxieties through ventriloquised monologues and dialogues spoken by inhabitants of this mythical place created by me.

My intellectual project, then, is one of complicating work that I find limited in some way so as to point to potentially more productive ways of thinking about a place or an idea. Though the price for this can be the charge of naiveté, revisionism or neo-colonialist thinking, this tendency to problematise or complicate has informed my thinking over a long time. In a contribution to an early collection of essays following the Grenada revolution entitled *Crisis in the Caribbean* (Nanton, 1983), I explored the regional crisis in the context of St Vincent's political economy, which showed a continued strong leaning towards conservatism in policymaking and outlook, leading me to pose the question: 'Crisis? What crisis?'. In an entirely different context, as a researcher and practitioner of race-relations policymaking in Britain, my concern was to challenge a one-strategy-fits-all approach to race policy formulation and implementation. For example, in a context of anti-racial-harassment policies, how might an equalities discourse access and monitor so-called black-on-black violence– for example the practice of robbing gold bangles from Asian women by black youth? Or, for that matter, the vexed question of who should adopt a black child – a devout black Pentecostal family or a white atheist one in a predominantly secular society like Britain? At a policymaking level, would the implementation of an equalities policy that suited an inner London suburb with a high black or minority presence be just as applicable and effective in a rural county council setting with a fraction of the relevant minority group (Nanton, 1984)?

No doubt the personal also plays a part in this problematisation project. I was born in St Vincent and educated in the 'metropolitan centre', i.e. Britain, in the course of which I returned to St Vincent as a Ph.D. researcher for fourteen months in 1979–1980. My aim was to study the transfer of power in a small Caribbean country: the role of the State in SVG. As a doctoral candidate I was expected to view the society through a sociological lens and do the things that a diligent student of sociology conducting fieldwork might do: collect data, conduct interviews, compare and contrast situations, and such. These plans were prepared some 3,000 miles away at the University of Sussex. I arrived, not to a sleepy Caribbean backwater, but to an island experiencing a major volcanic eruption, with the population of its northern half evacuated into schools, church halls, abandoned buildings and private homes in its southern half during the first eleven weeks of my return. The immediate disruption and knock-on effects continued for some time. This experience literally blew apart any preconceptions of my months-long prepared role as academic scholar and researcher. The St Vincent Government broadcasting authority, desperate for any sign of outside support, announced on the radio one day soon after my arrival that: 'In our hour of need Vincentian sociologist Philip Nanton has returned.' Flattering as this announcement sounded, the reality was considerably different. My role was to sit on the back of a lorry or two to ensure that donated foodstuffs from abroad were not stolen en route from Central Police Station to evacuation camps. I then had to bring together the conceptual lens that I had adopted with the material reality that I experienced on the ground.

My point here is that this experience armed me with a degree of scepticism about received wisdom and conventional discourse, including, for example, postcolonial theory. The experience also encouraged me in another sense – that is, to become my own organic case study. The personalised strategy adopted in this work, for better or worse, can be read as a response to that experience.

In the light of this admission, what then might a reader obtain from the eclectic mix of this work? I hope that the reader will obtain, firstly, an alternative paradigm with which to re-examine the Caribbean; secondly, a cross-disciplinary analytical tool – that of frontier study – that integrates and straddles the disciplines of history, geography, literary studies, and social and cultural analysis, with a view to opening up new avenues of discussion about the Caribbean and other frontier societies; and thirdly, a work offering a close examination of an under-researched multi-island Caribbean society, St Vincent and the Grenadines.

1

Pirates of the Caribbean: frontier patterns old and new

State marginalization and the region as hinterland

The anglophone Caribbean region has two distinct faces. One face, the one shown to the outside world, suggests 'everything cool', ease and even contentment. Democratic traditions (for the most part) are upheld, the sun shines, the rules of cricket are obeyed, tourist services are friendly and order is maintained. The parliament buildings in Barbados are the third oldest in the Commonwealth after Britain and Bermuda. Barbados is proud of its tradition of political stability. Apart from the nips of a few mosquitoes; some sunburn; and the drawn Test cricket series achieved when the England team visited St Kitts, Grenada and Barbados,[1] their supporters, the so-called 'Barmy Army', are unlikely to have been otherwise much disturbed by their visit. And there is modernity. In 1966 V. S. Naipaul drew attention to Trinidad's modernity.[2]

These images of calm, serenity, playfulness and modernity struggle to crowd out the region's other face of localised violence (increasingly gang-based and in run-down city locations) and disorder. In 2012 murder rates in Jamaica and tiny St Kitts and Nevis were among the ten highest in the world. In a region with an above-average rate for rape and sexual violence, such cases in St Vincent and the Grenadines (women raped and sexually assaulted) in 2011 reached 389 per 100,000 population compared to a global average of 15 per 100,000.[3] A recent review of gang violence in Trinidad offered the extreme suggestion that with an estimated 95 gangs and approximately 1,269 members, gangs have a stronger hold on the Trinidad population than its Government does

(Johnson, 2013). Direct defiance of the State is at its highest in 'garrison' communities, essentially urban, ghettoised islands of self-regulated groups policed and managed by gang lords.[4] These examples suggest a severe problem of self-governance. In addition the implementation of regulation and imposition of law and order are a challenge for the State, with knock-on economic and social effects for everyone.[5] It is, then, a region where an authoritative appearance of order and good govern-ance disguises dystopic elements suggestive of frontier and hinterland.

It should be understood that the Caribbean has had a long experi-ence of accommodating this darker, wilder side. Historically, the role of the State as a force for effective regulation has, for a number of rea-sons – economic practices, belief systems and patterns of migration – long been circumscribed. Accommodation of illegality and weakness of State institutions appear to go hand in hand, so when the State does lash out, its actions are often extreme: witness the periodic wholesale burn-ing of ganja fields and the military-style operation to arrest 'Dudus' Coke in Tivoli Gardens, Kingston as recent examples. To substantiate my claim that such incidents are evidence of surviving frontier pat-terns, I will first delve into some regional history. This offers a context for my claim that shifting state boundaries, strong privatisation, weak State regulation and social withdrawal are regional frontier features.

Shifting boundaries

Where to draw the geographic boundary between one territory and the next? This is a long unsettled question that raises its head period-ically in one location or another throughout the region. In the early colonial period the islands were traded like booty, to the extent that St Lucia, traded back and forth between France and Great Britain, became known as the Helen of the West Indies. More prosaically, even within the British area of rule, boundaries between one territory and another were periodically redrawn or challenged. In 1885, Barbados was removed from the British Windward Islands to be administered separately as a colony. In 1891 there were riots in Kingstown when it was rumoured that the Legislative Councils of St Lucia, St Vincent and Grenada were to be merged. After a brief flirtation with a federal structure in the 1950s, island-based political independence followed in various amalgamations (Trinidad and Tobago, St Vincent and the Grenadines, Antigua and Barbuda, St Kitts and Nevis etc.). Many of these island nation states, based on uneasy alliances, have been subject to threats of secession and the redrawing of state boundaries. Nevis's dispute with St Kitts is the latest illustration of this trend.

Emigration has presented another boundary challenge through the centuries. The earliest pressure on migration involved regional attempts to restrict the outflow of labour, in an attempt to maintain an adequate supply of cheap manpower in the islands. In the nineteenth century, many islands passed local Emigration Acts, imposing financial penalties on ships' masters for transporting passengers without the requisite certificates. However, given the geographical complexity of the region, with innumerable small cays throughout, for example, the Bahamas, Virgin Islands and Grenadines, implementation was not a simple matter. In the vicinity of St Vincent, the Grenadines became notorious as offering an easy route for ships to pick up illegal emigrants undetected. The lament of the lieutenant-governor of St Vincent on the difficulties of controlling the illegal migration of 1874 could easily be mistaken for that of a twenty-first-century regulator of illegal trafficking. In his dispatches he noted: 'The existence of these scattered islands with sheltered harbors stretching from St Vincent to Grenada make[s] it difficult to keep control over the Grenadines trade and hence the movement of vessels there.'[6] Many Leeward and Windward Islanders sought to migrate to more wealthy islands, especially Trinidad, Aruba and Curaçao to the south, which were, in turn, a gateway to Venezuela in richer times (Richardson, 1992).

Since the twentieth century out-migration has become an essential safety valve, offering relief from high levels of under- and unemployment in the region, cheap labour for the metropoles and substantial invisible export earnings. In Jamaica, where unemployment was esti-mated at about 15 per cent of the labour force in 1953, by the early 1960s emigration had probably reduced unemployment both relatively and absolutely (Tidrick, 1973: 191). Admittedly some aspects of the organisation of the out-migration were taken over by metropolitan and local elites through State institutions. However, the decision to migrate has always been that of the private individual. In global fron-tier terms, this supply of labour from the hinterland offered a suffi-ciently 'civilised' workforce to help fill the lowest ranks of industry and public services in the metropolis. This was a population, after all, who could speak English, French or Dutch, and who, for better or worse, had been intensively schooled, formally and informally, in British, French and Dutch ways.

One result of emigration has been that a defining characteristic of the late-twentieth-century Caribbean as a region is the growth of large (in proportion to the size of the remaining 'home' populations) island diasporas in western metropolitan cities. Ralph Premdas collated Cohen's data to demonstrate that by the 1980s in Britain there was a community of some 650,000 'Black Britons'. By 1990, 337,000 migrants had left the French Antilles for France and about 250,000 Dutch Antilleans had left for the Netherlands (Premdas, 2002: 58). A num-ber equivalent to well over two-fifths of the home population of Puerto Rico, Suriname, Martinique, Guadeloupe and Jamaica are now located in the traditional metropolitan centres of the USA, the Netherlands, France and Britain (Grosfoguel, 1995). Unofficial estimates suggest that a number equivalent to nearer 100 per cent of the home population of Barbados, St Vincent and Dominica, respectively, now live outside the 'home' society.

Where the State is politically independent, the diaspora population is, in practice, outside the sanction of the 'home' state. Premdas sug-gests that this extensive migration requires nothing less than a recon-ceptualisation of the role of the State. He notes that 'the practices of Caribbean peoples are at great variance from the exclusive claims for singular loyalty to the state ... Caribbean peoples share a common de-territorialised imaginary. This requires a re-conceptualization of the notion of sovereignty' (Premdas, 2002: 60). However, at the same time many people in Commonwealth Caribbean states rely on remittances from migrants abroad as essential private economic supplements. Remittances to Jamaica are estimated to amount to 4–5 per cent of gross domestic product (GDP) per annum; those to Guyana have been estimated at around USD90 million per annum, or 13 per cent of GDP. The small number who return 'home' to the region after many years are often culturally and socially alienated to some degree, and as a result, migrants of the 1950s and 1960s, returning from the UK after many years, were often characterised socially as 'mad' (Thomas-Hope, 1992). However, despite problems of re-engagement, returnees exercise sufficient influence for island governments like those of Jamaica and Barbados to woo them with periodic island association meetings in the Caribbean and to offer financial inducement packages on their return. For a small number of seasonal migrants (sports people, retired grandparents with diasporic offspring, seasonal agricultural workers) who divide their time between homeland and metropole, the official boundaries are a minor inconvenience.[7]

Another area where social boundaries shift and may be crossed and recrossed according to practice and belief is that of various forms of herb usage and consumption. Smoking marijuana, for example, has been recognised to be 'widely prevalent in the lower socio-economic groups in Jamaica for more than one hundred years' (Thorburn, 1974: 19). During this time the drug has acquired a long history of use as a spiritual herb among the Rastafarian religious sect and in more recent years its use has spread across the range of social classes. Possession of 2 oz or less in Jamaica, as noted below, has recently been legalised. In 2014 leaders of the Caribbean Community (CARICOM) instituted a study of the implications of marijuana legalisation.[8] There is also a whole institution of alternative medicine, directed by so-called bush-men, or herbalists, based on the belief that the spiritual body can fight off all possible ailments if strengthened by herbs. The practice is carried out through a mission, led by a mother or shepherdess of the 'balm-yard'. While many medicinal herbal teas are reported to be harmless and not illegal, 'several harmful examples' have been reported on in Caribbean scientific literature. One of the best known of these is the 'white back', or 'consumption bush' (*Crotalaria fulva*), which is widely consumed in Jamaica and causes vero-occlusive diseases of the liver (Lowe, 1972: 21).

These unofficial spiritual and health-related practices represent alternative belief systems. Some belief systems in the past – for example the practice of *obeah* – have been interpreted as a direct challenge to authority and have drawn a charge of sedition (Chevannes, 1971). The religious practice of the Shakers, or Spiritual Baptists, was banned in both St Vincent and Trinidad before being first tolerated and then welcomed. The issue here is that considerable areas of the unofficial social world of Caribbean belief and practice have continuously existed parallel with, or at times crossing, the boundary between legal and illegal, official and unofficial, wild and civilised worlds.

Religion and social withdrawal

Certain forms of religious adherence have, in contrast, triggered a quietist social withdrawal. For an increasing number of people in the Caribbean charismatic churches, involvement, in terms of belief system and practical support, has led to a supplanting of the State and secular politics. The Pentecostal churches are the sole exception to the decline in church attendance and claimed denominational adherence in each ten-year census for the past thirty years. The biblical principle of tithing has enabled them to grow rapidly, so that in St Vincent, by 2001, the Pentecostals were almost on a par with the island's traditionally dominant Anglican population, each with 17 per cent of the claimed church adherence. By 2012, the Pentecostals had almost doubled this percentage. These churches are demonstrably most popular among the poorest in Caribbean societies; but it's worth noting that those whose incomes are too low to be subject to State taxation are the very people who willingly pay tithes to the Church. In Diane Austin-Broos's study of the history and influence of the Pentecostal Church in Jamaica, where Pentecostals make up the largest single category of religious affiliation, she shows that in 1996 they supported 337 churches, maintained assets equivalent to around USD16 million, and sustained 632 pre-school centres and 2 old-age homes. Furthermore, the Church offers a retirement plan for ministers, funeral assistance and life insurance programmes. International links enable Church members from the Caribbean to obtain access to congregations in other countries, particularly Britain and the USA, where the parent churches originated. The ideological basis on which the world of Pentecostalism is constructed leads to the avoidance of involvement with the State. While adherents recognise the role of the secular State and its politics, they view them as peripheral. In Austin-Broos's words: 'They [Pentecostal churches] leave in their wake a distance from the state, and a quietistic response to politics. This response, moreover, is sustained and encouraged by links with the metropolitan world' (Austin-Broos, 1996: 63).

Strong privatisation and weak regulation

The State's weak regulatory role has gone hand in hand with disputed boundaries, uncertain scope and, just as importantly, privatisation in the widest sense (i.e. pertaining to the private sphere). In the seventeenth century, Caribbean islands seized by Britain quickly became a combination of frontier settlements for soldiers who expropriated them. When Jamaica, for example, was founded as a colony, the social historian Richard Pares noted that: 'It was laid out regiment by regiment, here we are told the regiment of Colonel Barry planted, and there the regiment of General Doyley' (Pares, 1960: 3) Central to this period is the early shaping of the region as a locale of lawlessness, piracy and gangsters through the tradition of privateers and buccaneers that was at its height in the 1660s. Philip Curtain noted its longevity when he observed that 'the last Caribbean pirate was hanged in the 1830s, the decade that brought emancipation to the British islands' (Curtin, 1990: 96). This time-honoured piratical tradition has not completely disappeared. The London-based International Maritime Bureau identified eight attacks on merchant ships in the Caribbean Sea in the first three months of 2003 (International Maritime Organization, 2004).

The history of plantation slavery has cast a long shadow of uncontrolled privatisation in the region. There were few regulations to inhibit this privatised process of 'wealth creation'. In the case of plantation slavery in Jamaica, Orlando Patterson has noted that: 'Power was completely diffused ... state and society were poorly developed, a bureaucracy hardly functioned and when it did was extremely inefficient'(Patterson, 1967: 93). Barry Higman's overall assessment of plantation slavery in the region, based on census data, is an indictment of the absence of regulation. The laissez-faire philosophy and harsh conditions of labour threatened the scope for a natural increase in population. He demonstrates that once supplies of slaves from West Africa were reduced, the population declined to such an extent that it was threatened with extinction. For the period 1807–1834 he points out: 'The central feature of the experience of the British Caribbean slave population was the general failure to achieve a natural increase, to show more births than deaths.' Although he identified significant variations in the level of natural increase in a few islands, he argues that: 'The continued harshness of the regimes under which the slaves laboured after 1807 made ultimate extinction a real possibility' (Higman, 1984: 4–5).

After the 1820s and the collapse of the second boom in the price of sugar, the fear of increasing costs resulting from the abolition of slavery, and growing difficulties in obtaining property sales of plantations encumbered by high mortgages and with the abandonment of certain estates, a dramatic change occurred, in perceptions of both the fabulously wealthy West Indian and the value of a close colonial relationship. The change leads once again to a less flattering view of the region: that of a metropolitan-dependent periphery, populated by various forms of colonial cheats and idlers, on whom 'civilisation' (never a given in a frontier society) needed to be imposed. Writing about his visit to the

West Indies in 1859, for example, the British novelist Anthony Trollope made repeated reference to the region's want of 'civilisation' and, on Jamaica's lamentable public institutions, Trollope noted 'of [their] public honesty – I will say nothing … but the Jamaicans speak of it in terms which are not flattering to their own land' (Trollope, 1859: 121).

One reason for increasing British suspicion was the worsening relationship between absentee landowners and their colonial dependants. Although this suspicion can be traced as far back as the seventeenth century, it intensified in times of economic decline. Whenever absentee landlords tried to make claims on their estates in the West Indian colonies, Richard Pares notes that: 'Nothing could altogether counteract the tendency of the colonial communities to favour the interest of the resident debtor against those of the creditor in Europe. Every creditor found that "*les absents ont toujours tort*"' (Pares, 1960: 44).

As already marginal Caribbean economies took a downturn in the last twenty years of the nineteenth century, a form of minimum welfare ideology became established. The first locally initiated land settlement policy in the British West Indies, aiming to provide land for the landless, was put into effect in St Vincent in 1885. This was one practical response to what was increasingly identified as 'the West Indian problem': poverty, unemployment and maladministration. Among many such reports, the *Report of the Moyne Commission*, compiled in the 1930s but embargoed till 1945 because of fear of social unrest, was the most well known. This welfare ideology was to expand, with the State taking increasing responsibility for 'development', after island states became politically independent from the 1960s.

With the economic collapse of sugar and the decline of the West Indies as a region of strategic importance during the nineteenth century, a fundamental change can be identified in the underlying economic structure of the society as well as in the way the region and its population were perceived. The private business sector, which for a long time relied on metropolitan protection of its export produce, became increasingly oligopolistic, with core sets of families in each territory moving out of agriculture into merchandising, controlling significant directorships and operating to influence the agenda of the State (Brown and Stone, 1976; Reid, 1980).

With political independence in the 1960s this reliance on the State continued, taking the form of exclusive Government contracts and import licences to prop up domestic markets (Henke and Marshall, 2003). Public sector spending increased dramatically, both in manufacturing and in government service provision. For a while relatively high rates of economic growth were achieved, enabling island governments to remain politically independent in spite of an increasingly globalised economic system.

The rise and decline of the status of marijuana as an illegal crop provides another illustration of both the continued dominance of the private sphere and the marginalised role of the State. A central feature of most twentieth-century Caribbean economies is their 'openness' and thus vulnerability to world economic trends, affecting illegal no less than legal cash crops. The pattern of economic expansion and contraction in the traditional cash-crop sector of Caribbean economies (bananas, sugar, spices, cotton) appears to have been duplicated in marijuana growing. Agricultural production for export has dominated the region from the outset, with small economies shifting over the centuries from one export cash crop to another, as they are overtaken by higher marginal costs because of their smaller scale of production than producers elsewhere. One important cause of the demise of sugar production in the nineteenth century, for example, was the onset of cheap mass production of sugar beet in Europe. In the eastern Caribbean, typical island products, such as finely woven sea-island cotton, cocoa and arrowroot, were each in turn threatened and then overtaken by more economical Egyptian cotton, West African cocoa and Egyptian arrowroot.

In the context of this pattern of early exploitation of a cash crop followed by its demise as larger producers enter the market, the recently attractive marijuana crop may become the latest casualty of this cycle of expansion and decline. Marijuana production appears to have reached a peak in the 1970s and is reported to have been in decline for the past two decades. By 2000, Caribbean marijuana was being replaced in its traditional export markets – the United States, Canada and the United Kingdom – by high-quality Mexican or Moroccan product. The 2000–2001 UNODC report argues that, in real terms, the value of Caribbean marijuana exports had plummeted by 80 per cent since the early 1980s. In the UK, herbal cannabis from the Caribbean was estimated to represent less than 2 per cent of the market (UNODC, 2003, 10). Its provenance today is essentially in intra-regional trade.

It would be misleading to suggest that after fifty or more years of political independence Commonwealth Caribbean states have become passive in areas of public policy such as social welfare provision, public sector education, health care and national insurance provision. Many Caribbean states have achieved middle-to-low ranking in the United Nations Development Programme (UNDP) Human Development Report for their efforts at inclusive public provision. By 2000, a handful had achieved high ranking (i.e. among the top thirty countries internationally), with Barbados and the Bahamas notably leading the 'medium' range of countries. Welfare ideologies promoting the legitimacy of the State are, however, over-shadowed by shifting boundaries, violence and the fear of violence, and social withdrawal, as well as a number of privatised traditions and institutions that centre on the individual. Furthermore, with political independence local State intervention policy has been at best variable and at worst ineffective, its capacity for regulation weaker and more circumscribed than official paradigms of illegality would suggest.

In the absence of close attention to popular and alternative structures, beliefs and practices, the gap between State exhortation and concrete action widens, and some paths to earning a living gain a liminal status where illegality is tolerated and, in some instances, respectability may eventually be achieved. In other frontier situations the process of imposing regulation itself becomes a minefield. Both instances suggest that frontier retentions remain common throughout the anglophone Caribbean. One of the most recent examples of the latter – comprising variable regulatory practices and shifting boundaries of regulation – is afforded by the development of the off-shore services industry, whereby Caribbean jurisdictions offer their services to the global financial community. This sector has become second to tourism in its importance to Caribbean economies and in 2011 accounted for 17 per cent of regional GDP. In more specialised international financial centres in the region (Bahamas, Barbados, Bermuda, Cayman Islands, British Virgin Islands) the value of this sector is estimated to be larger than 25 per cent, in value estimated to be a proportionate size larger than that maintained in Luxembourg.

These jurisdictions provide a range of off-shore banking services: the establishment of international companies as well as trust services to international clients interested in taxation benefits and estate planning. Western governments, which have over time imposed more and more global rules on smaller Caribbean regimens, claim that alongside the legitimate users of these services weak regulations in Caribbean jurisdictions have facilitated a range of illegal practices that are invariably secret.[9] In 1989, following the G7 Summit in Paris, an international consortium of governments established a Financial Action Task Force to combat money laundering and financing of terrorism. Since the events of 9/11 regulatory requirements have intensified and a plethora of these instruments, some collective, others set up by individual western countries, have come into existence, forcing Caribbean countries into various levels of compliance. As the Caribbean now represents the fourth largest world banking sector, and the financial services sector is a major income earner for smaller territories in the region, the jurisdictions have considered it necessary to comply to ensure that they are recognised as respectable service providers in the global financial world. The Organisation for Economic Co-Operation and Development (OECD) countries operate three levels of 'non-cooperating countries and territories': 'black', 'grey' and 'white', in ascending order of transparency and legality. The frontier element of such services derives from the fact that regulatory processes continue to be negotiated and are in constant flux. Some analysts suggest that even among the metropolitan countries attempting to impose (their version) of order, there is an element of the wild. Secondly, information is limited about the size of the sector and how it operates.

A 2015 review of the sector in the anglophone Caribbean drew attention to the region's inability to attract dedicated training of its regulators by international agencies as a major source of concern. It appears that the rapid growth in the sector in the region frightened international agencies, which responded by imposing ever changing demands on the regulatory practices of Caribbean jurisdictions while offering harsh criticism of the region's inability to keep up.

The experience of St Vincent, one of the smaller jurisdictions offering these services, illustrates a particular form that the frontier nature of this world has taken. A recent review indicated that this country's off-shore sector was devoid of any regulators. Its pugnacious style in attracting international customers appeared to take on the world. For example, following the passage of the St Vincent and the Grenadines International Business Companies (Amendment and Consolidation) Act 2007 (Section 97) international investors and their professional advisors were pitched the offer of protection from 'greedy spouses and inconsiderate creditors' through the internet. It was suggested that St Vincent's legislation protects a St Vincent-registered international company and so 'kicks in where a foreign court attempts to adjudicate on issue of title to shares'.[10] This hustler's pitch, one among a number (including the 'SVG hybrid company' offering protection so that 'unwanted attention from onshore revenue authorities is avoided'), offers a direct challenge to other regulatory regimes. Essentially it is argued that St Vincent law offers non-recognition of foreign judgments in the case of SVG Trusts. In 2000 St Vincent was on three 'black' lists, removed from the OECD list of tax havens in 2002, but 'grey'-listed for a year in 2009. It may, of course, be a coincidence, but in 2008 St Vincent amended its Banking Act, tightening the regulatory regime for banks in St Vincent, and repatriated control over international banks to the International Financial Services Authority. Soon after there was a sharp drop in the number of off-shore banks operating in the jurisdiction: from forty in 2001 to seven after the legislation was passed in 2008.

The fairness or otherwise of costly metropolitan-imposed global requirements on small countries remains a hotly disputed topic. For the most part Caribbean countries have responded to many of these regulatory demands to enable them to remain globally respectable. However, complicating the frontier issue, the metropolitan centres that make and seek to enforce the global rules of good international financial centre practice have themselves been indicted for having a worse record than small state international financial centres, particularly in the establishment of shell companies.[11] Perhaps limits have been tested, the act is being cleaned up and this process will continue. But we should not be too spiritual. There seems to be a place for identifying a continuum of wildness or frontier in this sector, whether in the Caribbean or worldwide. Jurisdictions will find themselves at different points along that continuum depending on the situation.

Jamaica Kincaid succinctly sums up a popular sense of the spirit of frontier in an interview in the *New Yorker* where she discusses the collapse of Allan Sandford's bank in Antigua, a financial disaster for his international depositors as well as many local Antiguans. Linking the experience back to the region's early history, she observes:

> In Antigua there's always a man, a person who comes in from the rest of the world – a pirate. Piracy is very close to Antiguan history. They have been coming and hiding money and stealing for hundreds of years. This man comes to Antigua and corrupts the place, and everyone's happy because they're making money. The ones who aren't benefiting from it, like me, are the opposition.
>
> (Wilkinson, 2009)

In this chapter it may seem that I have played fast and loose with the term 'frontier'. If so, it has been to register what I see as the legitimacy of the term's continued use in a variety of arenas across the Caribbean region. I have noticed calmness and order alongside violence and mayhem. I have noticed that V. S. Naipaul has hinted at modern/primitive tensions. In the context of Caribbean history, real politics and political economy the word slips and slides: at times the frontier suggests a moveable state border line; at others it suggests a 'boundary' in the expanded sense of zone. It also extends to a notion of 'testing the limits' of order and civility. But enough of the *apologia*: load your supplies, ready your rifle and cartridges, and hitch your horses to the wagon. In the chapters that follow we will use that small but complex star, the nation state of St Vincent and the Grenadines, as our touchstone and guide in exploring more precisely the many features of Caribbean frontiers, old and new.

Notes

1 The series of three Test matches was held in April and May 2015.
2 'Trinidad', he notes, 'considers itself, and is acknowledged by the other West Indian territories to be, modern'. The characteristics of 1960s modernity he enumerates include night clubs, restaurants, air-conditioned bars and the like, including a strong American influence. But these observations on Trinidadian modernity would not be Naipaulian without a sting in the tail; he recollected also: 'when I was a boy not to know the latest commercial jingle was to be primitive' (Naipaul, 1996, 39–40).
3 UNODC (2007): see table headed 'Sexual Violence'. Unfortunately, St Vincent's sad achievement here was not worth a comment in the more optimistic overview of violence in the region provided by UNODC (2012). Antigua's spike of 100 rapes per 100,000 in 2007 was the highest recorded and discussed in a context that suggested that small increases in societies with small populations exaggerate the indicator (26).
4 For an example of a violent, frontier-style operation by the Jamaican military and its aftermath in one such location see the story of the capture of Christopher 'Dudus' Coke in May 2010 (Schwartz, 2011).
5 The 2007 UNODC report on violence in the Caribbean indicated that were Jamaica and Haiti to reduce their rates of homicide to the level of Costa Rica, each country would see a growth rate of 5.4 per cent annually (UNODC, 2007).
6 Memo from William Hepburn Rennie to [?] Lawson, 30 March 1834, Public Record Office, London, CO 260/37.
7 Nearly twenty years ago Aaron Segal identified this pattern of regular movement; see Segal (1996).
8 They established a Regional Commission on Marijuana to inquire into the social, economic, health and legal issues surrounding marijuana use in the region and to advise on reclassification. The issue was introduced by Ralph

Gonsalves, the Prime Minister of St Vincent and the Grenadines. Jamaica had recently decriminalised the possession of up to 2 oz of the drug if used for religious, scientific or medical purposes.

9 R. T. Naylor's *Wages of Crime: Black Markets, Illegal Finance and the Underworld Economy* paints the following picture of how this process operates. He states: 'the most fundamental rules in money laundering are to avoid contact between the bank account and the data bases police are known to search, to use private mail drops, and to keep one's mouth shut. These rules also demand that illicit money be held not by an individual (even in a "numbered" account) but by a corporation. Therefore before sending money to the haven of choice, the launderer will probably call on one of the money jurisdictions that sell offshore corporations, that is, corporations licensed to conduct business only outside the country of incorporation, free of tax or regulations and protected by corporate secrecy laws.' Naylor notes that the traditional favourite locations for these practices have been Liberia, the Cayman Islands, the British Virgin Islands and Panama (Naylor, 2002: 161).

10 See Legair (n.d.).

11 See Sharman (2011).

2

Locating the frontier in St Vincent and the Grenadines

Kingstown panorama

A pirogue slices the morning sea, bouncing from wave to wave. A fisherman sits in the stern, one hand on the tiller. The pirogue is powered by an outboard engine. The man leans forward, crouching against wind and sea-spray, gauging each oncoming swell. A thin 'V'-shaped wake spreads from the bow across the deep-blue, choppy water. His partner sits facing him. They wear rough, well-used trousers, old shirts under bright yellow plastic jackets. Hats are jammed low on their heads. They do not speak. The man nearest the bow stares inland. He sees the curve of the bay. It snuggles below towering headlands to east and west. Behind the bay lie a range of folded hills.

If he had binoculars trained inland, the fisherman would see to the west a fort looming above the bay, black cannon rusting in their embrasures trained seaward. He knows that just as many cannon face inwards, away from the sea. Below, under their protection, red-roofed houses and shops made from wood or concrete with blue, yellow and pink walls, and a few churches, are packed together. They spread inland and along the bay's coastline joined by narrow winding lanes. Open gutters carry a thin stream of grey waste-water through the narrow lanes. Where the gutters are blocked the waste forms a stagnant trail of off-white scum. More houses dot the deeper green hills behind the town. Cooking smoke curls from a few chimneys. Some of the streets and pavements of the town are made from cobblestones and some from concrete or asphalt. They are all roughly constructed. There are gaps between each cobblestone from years of use and poor maintenance. The asphalt has thick patches that form low mounds, and in places it undulates unevenly. Many houses over-hang the pavements, supported by stone arches. The arches are a practical load-bearing solution to upper storeys. They provide shade from a fierce sun that will soon be overhead. They have become a small city's claim to a unique feature.

A drunk lies in a disused shop doorway surrounded by the acrid smell of piss and alcohol. (There is probably a law against this sleeping-it-off in public. There are no shortages of laws. Their implementation is always capricious.) He wears a loose, torn shirt that has seen better days. His trousers are encrusted with dirt. The thick white soles of his feet are without shoes. His head is wrapped in an old jute sack sandwiched between two thin pieces of cardboard. A few people pass him on their way to serve in a master or mistress's house, or to clean shops and offices. Cars begin to fill the streets and by mid-morning parking in the capital will be impossible. In the covered market, traders set up their tables to display their produce. Emaciated mongrel dogs play-fight near the vegetable market while they wait for scraps of food. Kingstown is awake.

The Caribbean frontier: a framework

Conventional frontier analysis takes the frontier as an aspect of the past, associated traditionally with disputed boundary lines and zones of conflict. It is either specifically identified or, if understood as a zone, of limited duration. Thus, for example, Howard Lemar and Leonard Thompson, in their introduction to *The Frontier in History: North America and Southern Africa Compared*, define the frontier as 'a territory or zone of interpenetration between two previously distinct societies'. The frontier 'opens', they suggest, 'when representatives of the intrusive group arrive, and "closes" when a single political authority has established hegemony over the zone' (Lemar and Thompson, 1981: 7). The frontier is either open or it is closed – though closure may take a while. The implication for St Vincent then is that once British hegemony was established the frontier was closed. Caribbean historians appear to agree with this perspective and have mostly consigned frontier analysis to the past. For example, Gordon Lewis, bemoaning the lack of scholarship in the region based on the concept of the frontier, identifies as his first diagnostic characteristic of Caribbean societies that 'they were in brief (and among other things) frontier societies' (Lewis, 1968: 4). Woodville Marshall, in his 1999 historiography of the Windward Islands, notes that after 1815, while they shared the common British colonial fate of many islands in the region, '[S]ome of them were briefly perceived as a frontier for plantation expansion' (Marshall and Brereton, 1999: 565).

Frontiers are, for historians it seems, either open or closed. One reason for this is that their essential understanding of frontiers appears to be driven by an ideological commitment that is region- or nation-state-focused. The essays in Lemar and Thomson's collection offer regional comparisons – North America and Southern Africa – or comparisons that involve fully formed nation states with fixed boundaries: United States of America, Canada or South Africa. In the Caribbean context, Gordon Lewis, much of whose work focuses on Puerto Rico, outlines this nationalist leaning regionally in 'Main Currents in Caribbean Thought', where he traces the progress of Caribbean thought, from pre-slavery through anti-slavery ideology towards nation state formation, concluding with the growth of nationalist thought (Lewis, 1983).

More specifically, the brevity of the frontier period in the Caribbean, according to Lewis, is a result of the imposition of slavery in these societies. Thus he rejects Fredrick Jackson Turner's frontier claim that: 'Since the days when the fleet of Columbus sailed into the waters of the New World, America has been another name for opportunity' (Lewis, 1983: 82). Lewis recognises frontier traits of rough democratic forms of government, hard drinking and rudimentary political structures as applicable to such locations as Yucatan logwood settlements of the seventeenth and eighteenth centuries. However, these forms, he argues, had disappeared by the late eighteenth century, overwhelmed by repressive and authoritarian slave society. For Lewis, then, Turner's attention to the opening up of opportunity, American distinctiveness and the scope of self management that the frontier offered could not apply to the Caribbean, which experienced, for centuries, a functioning industrialised slave society, albeit based on agricultural production. This perspective also implies that the social arrangements around the frontier in the Caribbean context have received little attention.

The approach to analysing the frontier adopted here is closer to Alistair Hennessy's more open and diverse understanding of the frontier (Hennessy, 1978). In his *The Frontier in Latin American History* Hennessy recognises in frontier studies scope for, among other things, understanding a rich diversity of material (when available), an explanation of peripheral capitalism as well as insularity. Frontier study also offers a useful foil to the nationalist representation of history. This notion of frontier can encompass an American sense of open-endedness as well as the more European idea of (fortified) boundary lines. This definition is useful to my exploration of the specificity of the frontier in a relatively under-explored Caribbean context, the eastern Caribbean island state of SVG.[1]

On the face of it, a society like SVG, one that develops from a traditional plantation base, has little reason to develop or extend a frontier analysis. It was part of a region where, in John Stewart Mill's words, 'England [found] it convenient to carry on the production of sugar, coffee and a few tropical commodities' (Mill, 1968: 320). It was a late-colonised, enclave economy comprising a hilly tropical island with a main port, dependent on foreign capital and in many ways pursuing economic activities unrelated to its locality. However, as Hennessy points out, to establish plantation institutions required traditional frontier expansion that was characterised by physical displacement and cultural deprivation, including physical uprooting. The plantation was also associated with maroon opposition as well as later labour resistance and rebellion. As St Vincent, like many British Caribbean societies, became a combination of welfare-dependent and service-industry enclaves, did the frontier simply disappear?

Far from disappearing, I am suggesting that the frontier remains very much present, if an under-recognised element of Caribbean island culture. Its traits are located in the restless and adventurous coastal wanderings of the Caribbean fisherman, sailor or sea-port smuggler. They can be found inland in the island-wandering woodcutter; those who squat on Government land; the urban dame school-teacher; or more recently, the innovative doctor, the mountainside ganja grower and in the financial services sector. I suggest also that the relevance of frontier study to the region has been resuscitated by international tourism's search for the exotic and the remnant 'wild' in the Caribbean. In this search for 'paradise' and expensive exclusivity St Vincent's even tinier Grenadine appendages – Bequia, Mustique, Canouan, Petit St Vincent, Palm Island and the Tobago Cays – are important new elements in the Caribbean frontier.[2] Biographies and autobiographies about Vincentians are in thrall to the metaphor of the pioneer or trailblazer.[3]

The purpose of this book, then, is to challenge the suggestion that the Caribbean frontier had a brief life and then was over. The concept of the frontier that is generally associated with the era of colonial conquest has continuing, and under-explored, analytical purchase in the context of the Caribbean region. Important traces continue to be found and new aspects to be identified. To demonstrate this survival and renewal I extend the conventional notion of frontier as physical boundary to suggest that, beyond physical boundary, the frontier holds also moral and ideational tension as the site of balance between what are imagined as 'civilisation' and 'wilderness'. I will suggest also that social movements challenge attempts to establish firm boundaries between notions of wilderness and civilisation. These last are slippery concepts, not least because while 'civilisation' is continually being revised as a conceptual tool, there is a tendency for 'wilderness' to disappear altogether. I argue, on the contrary, that the two are symbiotic: 'wilderness' is necessarily implicated in any discussion of 'civilisation'.

It is therefore important to attempt a definition of the terms. I understand 'civilisation' to refer to societal order and organisation that has some element of ideological imposition and artifice. The anglo-phone Caribbean is a region located in the Americas, but for the most part manifesting Western European ways of thinking. The region has experienced a long history of globalised enslavement, indentured and free labour, and raw-material exploitation since the fifteenth century European arrival. As a result, the Caribbean was probably the first (agriculturally) industrialised region of the globalised, capitalist western world, and through this incorporation combined colonialism with modernity. Over the long term it has undergone a gradual evolution in political systems, from various degrees of colonial dependency to territorial sovereignty. The result for the past sixty years has been the bequeathing of state management to a predominantly black and (particularly in Trinidad and Tobago and Guyana) East Indian political class controlling a host of individual islands and smaller island groupings of various sizes: among the latter is SVG, a politically independent multi-island state. The process of modernity arising initially out of colonisation is the beginning of what some may identify as 'civilising' practices that prioritise 'development'. From the perspective of those who hold power, who mobilise the label of civilisation or who are sufficiently dazzled by that power, the notion represents the best model of the present and the future. Ideologically it is a model that any 'sane' or 'reasonable' human being would embrace and applaud.[4]

'Wilderness' from the perspective of the 'civilised' is associated with raw nature, the absence of imposed order, and as a threat to that order. Thus, as Robert Frazer Nash observes, wilderness is not only a physical location, but also a state of mind. A wilderness is 'not so much what a place is but what men and women think it is. The New World was also a wilderness at the time of discovery because Europeans considered it so' (Nash, 2001: 7). Wilderness represents the untameable that always encroaches and may take a variety of forms. At the collective level I explore some of these forms of wilderness in SVG through the processes of social dislocation, the religious grouping formerly called the 'Wilderness People' and illegal marijuana farming in the northern St Vincent hills. At the micro level I use certain details of individual biography and monologue to draw attention to the ways in which the relationship between wilderness and civilisation is far from static but ever present and continually shifting. I am suggesting, then, that frontier may be read both as a process at the collective level and as a site of individual self-determination.

But the frontier has historically been and remains very much a part of global production. For example modern globalisation has shaped the development of various types of island tourism, from yachting to the discovery and development of discrete private island enclaves – the development of the Caribbean's financial sector as well as patterns of Caribbean migration. All of these developments I connect to notions of the civilised and the wild. The frontier, then, can be read as a form of moral landscape, an important element of which implies some form of boundary, where notions of civilisation and wilderness meet and regularly clash. In this sense, the frontier is a liminal space holding the other two structures in balance. In the Caribbean context, the continuation of frontier-influenced ideas can be perceived in the now commonplace notion of 'Caribbean civilization', variously and loosely defined (see Chapter 3 below). For ideological and aspirational reasons – driven variously by the Afro-centric reaction to centuries of racial denigration and the desire of post-independence leaders to demonstrate their own modernity – critical or analytical interest in Caribbean civilisation's dialectical counterpart, the 'wild' or 'wilderness', has been muted. The following section examines how, historically, this lacuna has come about and I will go on to illustrate collective and individual frontier retentions as well as new directions for the concept of the frontier in the region.

In bringing together the notions of civilisation and wilderness a fundamental question is how to apprehend the flexible and fluid nature of the 'frontier' in the Caribbean, and, in particular SVG. A region of such complexity offers a variety of ways to apprehend the notion of 'the frontier' and its sometimes overlapping and sometimes synonymous terms, 'border' and 'boundary'. An immediate if sometimes overlooked complication is that the region is located in the Americas and so subject to Fredrick Jackson Turner's special-case plea for the specificity of the 'American' frontier: that is, a line that moved east to west to create a cultural zone. Yet, simultaneously, the term is inflected by a regional tradition of European-influenced thinking. The European burden of meaning has traditionally rested on the notion of fixed borders between states. The North American tradition suggests broad regions of interaction involving more than one culture. Thus, the American and European traditions pull the meaning of 'frontier' in different directions.

Along with this tension the frontier, as common-sense 'category of practice' boundary-line delimiting one mini-state from another, has severe limitations in the Caribbean. Chapter 1 has demonstrated the appeal of redrawing these mini-state lines. At the other extreme, beyond the demarcation of state sovereignty, the multi-island mini-state of SVG affords a heady mixture of land and sea that further complicates (and even confuses) notions of boundary (line) and terrain (zone). For example, in the Grenadine ward islands that are part of the State of SVG the diligent 'collect and classify' analyst is confronted by a plethora of geographically locatable though mind-boggling sea/land frontiers between one island and another. In 1950, confronted with this array of 'islets' as he chooses to call them, Patrick Leigh-Fermor abandons the prosaic. He captures the other-worldness of the Grenadines archipelago in exalted, empathetic prose when he takes an aeroplane ride over the area, observing:

> innumerable islets scattered across the sea from horizon to horizon, and seeming, as they slid slowly southwards, to writhe and change shape and turn over: violoncellos, scissors, earwigs, pairs of braces, old boots, cogwheels, armadillos, palettes, wishbones, oak leaves, boomerangs and bowler hats, all of them hanging mysteriously in a blue dimensionless dream.

Alongside these, he notes: 'Solitary cones rose portentously through the penumbra, but no little wreathes of foam surrounded their crests; only a few yards of water separated them from the water-level. Pathetically, after so much uphill work, they had just missed being islands – "Well tried", one felt like murmuring' (Leigh-Fermor, 2005: 197).

However, without the luxury of the travel writer's metaphors, how might the analyst capture the array of frontiers encountered in the geographic confines of this nation state? Various stretches of sea water divide the so-called mainland island, St Vincent, from the Grenadines – the latter comprising inhabited and uninhabited islands and, as Leigh-Fermor suggests, mere rocks that lie just below or jut out of the sea.[5] A collective sea/land territorial boundary can legitimately be identified between the grouping of Grenadine islands and the St Vincent 'mainland' – this demarcation is given some legitimacy in the way that the nation state is officially named – St Vincent *and* the Grenadines. Some, but not all of the Grenadine islands are legitimate ports of entry to the State of SVG.[6] Yet another frontier between St Vincent and the Grenadines is geological – the Grenadine islands are geologically older than the volcanically formed St Vincent mainland. In contrast, while the island state of Grenada to the south of SVG includes two island dependencies – Petit Martinique and Carriacou – their existence is not acknowledged in the naming of that state. In the SVG context yet another line of sea/land territorial demarcation exists between each island in the national chain and its immediate surrounding seaboard – that of language. Thus Bequia, with some 5,000 year-round residents, 14 km (8 mi) south of St Vincent and the single largest island in the Grenadines chain, exhibits sufficient linguistic distinctiveness for linguists to conclude from a recent study of Creole English spoken there that 'there is a great deal that is unique to Bequia. The uniqueness is most evident in the discussion on the words and ways of speaking which, even if they are shared with other varieties of Caribbean English, often show unique meanings and usage on Bequia' (Meyerhoff and Walker, 2013: 119).

Beyond these administrative, territorial and cultural island-to-island distinctions, the concept of frontier as zone is further complicated when combined with the ambiguous concept of *islandness*. Chris Bonjie captures this ambiguity well in his observation that: 'The island is a figure that can and must be read in more than one way: on the one hand as the absolute particular, a space complete unto itself ... on the other as a fragment, a part of some greater whole from which it is in exile and to which it must be related ... it is a site of double identity – closed and open' (Bongie, 1998: 18). Furthermore, every island with a beach – and most have several – harbours a liminal space. Adam Nicholson, in his study *The Mighty Dead: Why Homer Matters*, calls the beach 'the great zone of liminality between land and sea, the sphere of chance-in-play'. He points out how symbolically potent is the departure of a vessel from a beach in Homer, and how often it occurs. Why? Because 'Leaving a beach is moving off from indecision' (Nicholson, 2014: 30).

In frontier terms islands may be small; simple they are not.

The more flexible concept of frontier as zone can to some extent respond to Bonjie's complication. Here the notion of frontier is also an intellectual and collective space that, as Nash suggests, exists in the imagination. The frontier here describes more a cultural and spatial zone that need not necessarily be fixed geographically. Of course, the temptation for island-discoverers, colonists and island nation-state managers (politicians and bureaucrats) to close the frontier is strong. This form of frontier closure is represented in the processes of mapping, naming, building and changing island landscapes, all of which are acts of possession – often presented for hegemonic purposes by colonialists as 'natural' and 'innocuous'. These actions are, as Rebecca Weaver points out, the characteristic behaviour of anyone who finds themselves stranded on an island. As she observes about imperial islands: 'Castaway colonists spend much of their time trying to turn (their location) into a more "civilized" Western space like that they left' – the great literary exemplar, of course, being Robinson Crusoe (Weaver, 2007: 24). This involves building huts, pens, bridges, gardens, as well as performing various other rituals of possession to make the place feel familiar. The antithesis of such behaviour, of course, is the process of 'going native'. Even when this does not occur, if the island is already populated at the time of 'discovery' a Man Friday is invariably involved as a mediator, and it would be misleading to think that all castaways and settlers necessarily invest to the same extent in the modernising and 'civilising' process.

Indeed, a challenge to the hegemonic process of possession is represented by Walter Mignolo as 'critical border thinking'. That is, a process whereby a cultural zone not only reflects modernity but is also critical of modernity. In this process of criticism the centre – more than likely 'colonial-managed', may be challenged at both the individual and collective levels. For Walter Mignolo this involves a process of 'epistemic rupture' and moments in which 'the imaginary of the modern world system cracks' (Mignolo, 2000: 73). From my local analysis of SVG it is unlikely that the grander rupture to the world system will be traced to Vincentian subaltern practices,[7] though cracks at the St Vincent level are not to be excluded. As I will demonstrate in the SVG case, the cracks or threats to the system that appear at the local level have, in these modern, populist times, invariably led to State strategies of incorporation, or a leaning in that direction. However, I borrow Mignolo's perspective, which I read as expressing an exploration of local thinking *from* the (wild side of the) border as well as thinking *about* the border from the 'civilised' side, to explore frontier behaviour at a local level in SVG. The study addresses those who, in Mignolo's phrase, see themselves as having no option but to challenge the power-centre and take an alternative direction. This challenge is issued through direct or indirect criticism of those, whether local or international, who presume to navigate the society and define the frontier. In this context, the hegemonic centre (characterised by 'civilised' thinking about the border) upholds 'common sense' and ultimately what those at the centre of power, on or off the island, identify as 'civilised' behavior. How these zonal frontier-challenge processes happen and how they work themselves out in the SVG context are the meat and drink of the chapters that follow. The attractiveness of the frontier concept in an island situation like SVG is precisely this double-edged potential for ambiguity. It can be envisaged as liminal, closed and open at the same time.

Central to this open/closed status of the frontier in the Caribbean is the additional notion of 'incompleteness'. This sense of incompleteness applies to both sides of the Caribbean frontier – the 'wild' and the 'civilised'. The frontier process that I am conjuring can be likened to the parodic and creolised 'New World Vision' threshold on which Wilson Harris locates Joseph Conrad's novel *Heart of Darkness*. Harris describes this vision as 'a complex wholeness inhabited by other conferring parts that may have once masqueraded as monolithic absolutes or monolithic codes of behavior in the Old Worlds from which they emigrated by choice or by force' (Harris, 1981: 87). He suggests that in the modern, globalised world the masquerade of cultural integrity needs to be abandoned and recognition given instead to the 'incompleteness' of each of the cultural elements that go towards making up the creolised whole (cited in Bongie, 1995, 246). This complexity is what I see as constituting a *frontier process*, in which each element is constantly being made while challenging the other, but each remains always incomplete. Civilisation and wilderness, then, function alongside a notion of *islandness* as both a sense of completeness, and, conversely, of openness to whatever might wash up on its shores – and thus incompleteness.

But to return to the particular. My study employs three modes of enquiry – historical, sociological and literary. The last of these three comprises monologues, poetic voice and literary criticism. In ranging across these genres I read the frontier from the perspective of the Caribbean island colony with its various geographical and cultural specificities, its hierarchies based on intimidation and imposed by a dominant capitalist world system. I argue that the concept of the frontier is essential both to Caribbean colonial history and to the Caribbean present. More recent developments – long-term colonial consolidation, political independence and globalisation processes – should not be allowed to obscure the frontier process in the Caribbean, which has never completely disappeared, and of which individual and collective traces remain. In the rest of this chapter and in Chapter 3 which follows I discuss the historical elements of 'civilisation' and 'wilderness' and the way that they have developed in SVG. In Chapter 4 I will examine at the micro and individual level three sketches of modern individual frontier lives in SVG. And at the collective level, I will demonstrate how competition over what I describe as 'the remnant wild' has become central to development in St Vincent's Grenadine dependencies. In Chapters 5 and 6 respectively I will discuss how this frontier collection of islands has been written about and how some of its (internal) cultural and social boundaries have shifted. The final chapter will examine the utility of frontier analysis for the study of islands in general, and implications for the study of the Caribbean and SVG in particular.

St Vincent and Kingstown's role in the frontier

There are many historical indicators of SVG's conventional frontier features – conflict over territory, colonial acquisition, outpost status and distance from any centre.[8] Kingstown, the imperially named capital, lies on the south-west coast between two towns with Kalina (Carib) names: Barrouallie to leeward and Calliaqua further to the south. Sandwiched between them, the *Kings* town embodies its frontier status, backed by hills, looking out to sea and facing down these Carib settlements.[9] Every feature of Kingstown speaks to its strategic and defensive role, starting with its location on a wide bay stretching 2.4 km (1.5 mi) across from east to west, and able to be defended against attack from sea or land, since the surrounding hillsides provided good sites for lookout areas and gun emplacements. In 1784, durable fortifications for Kingstown began to be built. By the last year of the Brigands' War the town's outer environs bristled with troops and gun emplacements facing both seawards and inland.[10] To the east was Cane Garden, where Three Gun Battery was located. To the west of the town separating Kingstown from New Edinboro stood One Gun Battery. Above this at about 600 feet (183 m) above sea level stood the garrison, Fort Charlotte, named after George III's consort. Fort Charlotte contained barracks for 600 men and 34 pieces of artillery of different descriptions. The fort was garrisoned till 1873 when troops were finally withdrawn from the island. On Dorsetshire Hill, to the north above the town, there stood a further garrison. The town also operated a militia of all freemen aged between 18 and 55, comprising 909 men ranging in rank from 2 Colonels to 785 rank-and-file members (Martin, 1843: 56).[11] In the centre of the town the House of Assembly contained two lookout or guard huts close to the road to afford a view of any mass movements converging on the seat of government. As the town slowly expanded from east to west around the bay the intention to provide security was clear. Meanwhile, the port offered a link by sea to the outside world.

Time for a song . . .

Song of Chatoyee

This is the land where I was nurtured
once beyond the British claim
green are our valleys
blue our mountains
places that I return again.

Every leaf, every bush
every branch on every tree
calls to Carib Chief. Cha-to-yee

This is the land that I fought for
here the place where I was slain
green are our valleys
blue our mountains
places that I return again.

This is the land my spirit wanders
coast to coast 'cross each terrain
green are our valleys
blue our mountains
places that I return again.

Every leaf, every bush
every branch on every tree
calls to me.

(Nanton, 2014b: 59)

Thus, in the late eighteenth century, the port of Kingstown was a colonial out-station where settler wagons could be circled, metaphorically, for protection.[12] They were opposed by the Garifuna (Black-Carib) population, an ethno-genesis grouping that combined over many years island Kalina (Carib) and ex-enslaved African-origin populations exercising pre-existing claims on the land and resisting colonial expansion.

The capture or sacking of the town was an important goal of their guer-rilla struggle. Though occasionally approached during the warfare this goal was never achieved.[13]

Along with the need for fortification, because of its remoteness and fear of Garifuna attack from land and French naval attack from the sea, other characteristics of Kingstown associated with the frontier include a rough and ready style of urban living – a kind of urban dereliction – as well as regular bouts of violent social unrest. In his 1837 *History of the West Indies* Robert Montgomery Martin estimates that Kingstown comprised only 300 'larger sized houses the lower stories of which are in general built with stone or brick, and the upper of wood, with shin-gled roofs' (Martin, 1837: 223). There were three main streets paral-lel to the sea. They were given the descriptively simple but practical names of Bay, Middle and Back Street. The rough and ready names of Middle and Bay Streets have persisted. Officially Back Street was later renamed Glenville Street in its eastern section and Halifax Street to the west, however its more informal name of Back Street persists. The main streets were intersected by six others. The early town pattern, laid out by the French during their occupation, has remained the basis of its street system, though where the French designated cobble-stoned Middle Street as the main street, the British preferred Back Street.[14] On Back Street there was a stone Court House used for Council and Assembly meetings on the first floor and below it the Court of Justice (Martin, 1843, 51). Three streams flowed through the town, with its red-roofed houses painted blue, yellow and pink.

Arrival at Kingstown port in 1826 involved few formalities. Frederick Bayley, a British travel writer who spent part of that year on the island, observed: 'There is no careenage at St Vincent ... instead of rowing gently alongside a flight of very convenient steps, and getting quietly out of the boat ... people are obliged to run their boats aground and ... leap onshore as soon as the sea may withdraw a respectful dis-tance' (Bayley, 1833: 171). Once ashore things hardly improved, since human pedestrians had to contend with untended pigs roaming freely in the heart of the town. The authority attempted to control them by urban slave gangs of 'old runaways [recaptured slaves] and generally hardened sinners' working in chains. It was one of their jobs to destroy every pig that they met: 'They cut off its head and threw the body in the roadside to be carried away by the owner' (Bayley, 1833: 196). Ten years later, the magistrate and journal keeper John Anderson painted a more general word picture of the town's dereliction, detailing

> The crazy wooden houses ... The badly paved, or metaled dirty streets, where broken bottles, – hoops of iron, & other rubbish lie huddled before the doors; the mean appearance of the low roofed stores and huckster shops; – the defaced & mouldering houses; the naked appearance of the planked, uncovered floors & walls of even the best and inhabited tenements.
>
> (McDonald, 2001: 63, 66)

An immediate reason for this lack of interest in urban public affairs was the limited commitment felt by white planter settlers to Kingstown beyond its function as a place of business and for protection. Throughout the nineteenth century colonial administrators continuously complained in their dispatches to the regional governor and to London about the maladministration of the governing planter elite in the House of Assembly. For example, by 1853 there was no regular system of taxation on the island and so taxes had to be voted annually in the island's House of Assembly. Assembly meetings were often poorly attended or simply not held. In January 1853 the recently arrived lieutenant-governor observed 'the Treasury was bankrupt, society disorganized and in fact I cannot better describe the situation of affairs than by saying that in all departments there existed a state of anarchy unexampled I believe in the history of this island'.[15]

It was on their plantation houses that planters chose to focus their attention, rather than public affairs or the town. In her *Domestic Manners*, Mrs Carmichael observed on her visit to St Vincent that 'The planters seldom come to the colonial town upon pleasure, and are always much occupied with their agricultural concerns, and anxious to return to their properties' (Carmichael, 1834: 19). Along with the centrality of the estate, Mrs Carmichael also observed the lavish entertaining that was on offer at one plantation house. She described in detail part of one spread for a dinner party for between thirty and forty guests: 'Turtle and vegetable soups, with fish, roast mutton and turtle dressed in the shell, with boiled turkey, boiled fowls, a ham, mutton and pigeon pies, and skewed ducks, concluded the first course' (Carmichael, 1834: 34).

For the white settlers who came from England, Scotland or Ireland, St Vincent was a place of exile. They were sojourners aiming to make a fortune before returning 'home'. In 1826, for example, when investment in sugar was paying high dividends, Bayley noted the particular meaning that the phrase 'at home' had for white Vincentian settlers.

> Unlike the inhabitants of the French colonies, they look upon the island in which they reside as a place to which they are, as it were, exiled for a certain period ... very few of them expect to die on those properties. Those who can afford it are in the habit of making trips every three or four years to the United Kingdom; and nearly all look forward to spending their last days in the land of their birth.
>
> (Bayley, 1833: 292)

This is borne out by remembrance plaques, dedicated to the society's nineteenth-century elite, covering the walls of Kingstown's St George's Anglican Cathedral. Commemorating men of wealth or status who held office in the island, as well as their loyalty to Britain, they name their far-flung final resting places as Kensal Green, London (for example Council Members James William Brown (d. 1847) and John Audain (d. 1864)); Berkshire (the Civil Service Commissioner George Herbert Dasent (d. 1876)); and south Wales (e.g. the planter John Whittall (d. 1858)).

The frontier is also traditionally associated with violence. In this respect, Kingstown was no exception. Once it was established as the island's foremost town, Kingstown became a place of security for members of white settler society and an important location where they sought protection against Garifuna fighters. Charles Shepherd describes one planter group embroiled in the Brigands' War as being 'obliged to take circuitous routes to avoid the high roads which were commanded by the enemy, to reach Kingstown' (Shepherd, 1831: 65). Long after British settlement, when planters and 'respectable folk' were sufficiently alarmed by protest of one form or another, they continued to seek refuge in Kingstown. The fear that drove them to the town changed from marauding Garifuna to their own dissatisfied estate labourers. For example, in 1862, in the wake of many grievances, labour unrest and rioting broke out on the island's Windward Coast estates. The historian Woodville Marshall, who has studied the causes and consequences of these riots, observes that: 'Planters clearly understood that they were targets; most of them "literally fled" when they heard of the assaults ... and did not return to their homes until the riots had been completely suppressed' (Marshall, 1981: 41–42). The *Barbados Globe* of the period reported: 'The greatest terror and consternation was felt in the countryside as well as in the towns, and most planters, whites and "respectable persons" immediately sought refuge in Kingstown from the rioters' demoniacal villainies.'[16]

However, this picture of Kingstown as the place of white planter refuge is not as simple as it appears. Before emancipation the social organisation of towns like Kingstown was characterised by contradiction and ambiguity. There was greater mixing than on plantations between enslaved and free, as well as across the whole range of class and colour.[17] The social mixing arose, as Barry Higman notes, because most of the slave population lived on the premises of their owners, though in separate rooms or out-buildings, while others lived in huts scattered among their masters' residences (Higman, 1995: 95). After emancipation the town increasingly became the space in which competing political interests of various sorts were worked out. Kingstown's streets became the battleground where protests were voiced, marches were held, and daily competition for space to live and trade remained at its sharpest. One indicator of this development, the historian Roderick McDonald notes, was that emancipation legislation reflected 'the high priority given to controlling apprentices'. He points out that this was reflected in new definitions of crime and criminality, and the introduction of new mechanisms of control such as the tread-mill.[18] The geographical area of Kingstown was part of John Anderson's responsibility as a stipendiary magistrate during the period of apprenticeship prior to the abolition of slavery. With more mobility among the general population, he records in his diary frequent brawls, drunkenness in taverns, illicit shebeens and debauchery in abodes of violence, as well as parties where stolen goods were consumed at town premises (McDonald, 2001: 101, 147). He refers specifically to the plundering of houses and provision grounds. Also commonplace was theft from ships landing cargoes like brandy, estate stores, butter and salt-fish.

Rioting in the town was recorded in the following years: 1838, 1841, 1855, 1856, 1858, 1862, 1879 and 1935. McDonald has analysed the repressive post-emancipation measures, including heavily punitive legislation to control Kingstown, and over-zealous magistrates, introduced by a fearful white political minority supported by the colonial administrative representative. He notes that by 1836 the number of prisoners on the island – 1,265 – was four times the annual pre-emancipation average. Kingstown had its own jail and house of correction. The measures, he argues, were introduced as an attempt to maintain white elite power by eradicating differences in the town between the free coloured community and black ex-slave apprentices (McDonald, 1996: 322). When the opportunity arose their introduction faced a backlash. At times the outcome of court cases was challenged by vocal groups who freed prisoners on their way to and from jail (Boa, 2002: 134), opposed the enforcement of judicial punishment by cat-o-nine tales (Marshall, 1981: 47) and challenged efforts to implement anti masquerading policies.[19] Often these actions in turn led to noisy, and sometimes violent, protests resulting in the calling out of the constabulary, the local (white) militia, and occasional colonial troop reinforcements sent from abroad. Sheena Boa, who has also studied the causes of some of these nineteenth-century Vincentian protests and their main participants, has shown that working-class women from Kingstown were often prominent in leading this unrest (Boa, 2002).

The idea of the frontier, long neglected in Caribbean studies with its frontier features of remoteness, defensiveness, violence, and a rough and ready society, can thus be seen as central to Kingstown's history.

Notes

1 SVG comprises a collection of thirty-two islands of varying sizes located between Grenada to the south and St Lucia to the north.

2 In his essay on the changing cultural geography of the frontier, an element of which is the contemporary wilderness experience, C. Michael Hall indicates that 'authentic, spiritual and escapist values are related to the cultural geography of the frontier and to strong elements of the "experience" that is commodified for the benefit of wilderness tourists' (Hall, 2002: 295).

3 See for example John (2009); King and King (2011). And see Chapter 4 below for discussion of two recent autobiographies of political pioneers.

4 Chapter 5 explores how this hegemonic model of civilisation, sometimes called 'Caribbean civilisation', is exploited by the political leadership in SVG, and Chapter 6 explores how it has been challenged.

5 Young's Island, Bequia, Mustique, Canouan and Union Island are all inhabited, and are different distances from the St Vincent mainland and from each other. The larger of the uninhabited rocks include Isle a Quatre, Balliceaux and Battowea. Some parts of the latter are privately owned while all of Mustique is leased to a private company that sets its own rules – for example only 140 houses may be built on that island at any time.

6 Bequia, Union Island and Canouan are legitimate ports of entry to the State of SVG but the inhabited island of Mayreau is not a port of entry.

7 However, the beginnings of a more robust regional 'epistemic rupture' may be detected in the collective confrontation between Caribbean states and ex-colonial powers, articulated in the growing demands for reparations for slavery.

8 In 1979 SVG became a politically independent, multi-island state comprising thirty-two islands, 389 km^2 (150 mi^2) in area. The islands for many years formed a minor part of British New World colonial island society.

9 Kingstown was not always the main town. First Barrouallie along the leeward coast and then Calliaqua were the centre of shipping. The latter served as a place for landing British military expeditions and reinforcements during the Brigands' Wars. In 1763, the island was acquired by the British at the Treaty of Paris. It was declared 'Crown property' and sold by auction to British subjects. Some 20,000 acres were 'given' to one Swinburne, while another 20,538 acres were auctioned to bidders. Some 4,000 acres were bought by General Monckton, who had earlier captured the island. The northern half of the island remained under Garifuna ('Black-Carib') control but soon became a site of a fierce contest among Garifuna, French and British interests. The

island was nominally governed from Grenada, first under Brigadier General Melville in 1763 and then under Leybourne in 1771. In 1776 it became sufficiently valued as exploitable plantation land for Valentine Morris to be appointed the island's first resident governor, presiding over a restless territory. Though Morris put much time, effort and his own money into island fortifications, his governorship ended in debacle when in 1779 the island fell to French invasion for a four-year period, for which he bore the brunt of the blame (Waters, 1964).

10 In two periods of fierce guerrilla warfare – 1772–1773, and then again in 1795–1796 – known as the Brigands' Wars, the island was the centre of intense bouts of conflict between the local Garifuna (Black-Carib) population who were supported by the French, in opposition to British forces. For details of the first Brigands' War see Fabel (2000). For the second Brigands' War see Jacobs (2003). From the settler perspective, they were converting underused land to sugar plantations. From the Garifuna perspective, settlers were denying them access to their own land on their own terms. Despite fierce resistance, by 1796, Chatoyer, the Garifuna Paramount Chief, had been killed and his followers routed. They were banished that year first to Balliceaux, a neighbouring islet off St Vincent where the shortage of food and water caused the death of around half the exiles. Of some 4,338 captives who entered Balliceaux between July 1796 and February 1797, a mere 2,248 embarked when expelled to Roatan, off Honduras, in March 1797 (Fraser, 2002).

11 These were the more standard defence forces. During the first Brigands' War they were supplemented by an additional British force of regular soldiers and marines who numbered close to 3,000, with around 2,000 slaves supporting these troops. Fabel claims these forces were opposed by only 500 Black-Carib guerrilla fighters. He describes the forces arranged against each other as 'a blow-torch to incinerate a wasp' (Fabel, 2000: 196).

12 In addition to these conventional features of a frontier, the composition of the island's population in the latter part of the eighteenth century is also characteristic of a frontier region. Of a total population of 13,603 in 1787, black/Africans made up 87.2 per cent, white/Europeans 10.6 per cent and the coloured/mixed a mere 2.2 per cent. The population geographer Joseph Spinelli suggests that the 10.6 per cent represented the highest proportion of white/European settlers at any time in St Vincent's history. The important frontier element to this statistic was its heavily skewed male-to-female ratio of 911 men to 126 women. Spinelli notes this feature 'was not out of reason for a frontier area, St Vincent had recently passed into British possession a mere 13 years earlier' (Spinelli, 1973: 323).

13 There were occasions in the skirmishes, between the Garifuna and their French backers on one hand and settlers and British military forces on the other, when this could easily have happened. This is because St Vincent was also a frontier society characterised by weak governance. Ivor Waters has described the island's first governor, Valentine Morris, as 'able'. But he notes that Morris was handicapped not only by Garifuna resistance. The exercise of State authority over settlers was resented. They objected to a 4.5 per cent tax

levy on exports as well as the requirement to contribute to the cost of naval protection. Waters claims that colonists were interested far more in looking to their own resources than in participating in the (white) militia (Waters, 1964: 37). Legislation required planters to keep one white person in the militia for every fifty slaves, under a penalty of £50 for each deficiency (Martin, 1843: 56).

14 Frederick Bayley describes Kingstown's layout in the early nineteenth century. Bay Street, the port landing area, was the centre of commerce. He notes: 'All the principal stores are in the bay, and the chief commerce of the island is there carried on.' Middle Street, he observes, 'contains but a few goods stores, and those chiefly for dry goods; there are, however, a number of little shops for the sale of caps, ribbons, and other articles of ladies' dress, which are generally kept by colored people. Also retail rum shops in abundance are therein contained; therefore there are always a number of sailors in the middle street.' Back Street he describes as unpaved, with 'a few stores in it, and the houses … chiefly the residences of those who are not engaged in commercial affairs … This street is moreover adorned with the residence of his Excellency, the Governor[, the] court house, the church, the methodist chapel, and the government house' (Bayley, 1833: 192–193).

15 Memo from Richard Graves MacDonell to William MacBean George Colebrook, 18 January 1853, Public Record Office, London, CO 260/79.

16 *Barbados Globe*, 13 October 1862, Bridgetown.

17 In Kingstown in 1817 there were estimated to be 2,255 people in slavery, representing 9 per cent of the colony's total slave population. Women constituted a high proportion of the working population in the capital, with some 41 per cent of the urban slave population registered as domestics (Higman, 1995: 228). By 1834 official records indicate that there were between 1,000 and 1,500 town-based slaves. Their employment extended to the wharfs, shipping or related vocations (382), non-praedial tradesmen (212) and domestic slaves (2,199) attached to households of the urban white population, with the remainder classified as 'aged, diseased or otherwise non-effective' (British Sessional Papers: House of Commons, 1835, Vol. L, 685, cited in McDonald (1996), 320).

18 In 1821 was passed "An Act for Building a Cage, and for establishing a Police in the Town of Kingstown", followed six years later by 'An Act for the Establishment and Regulation of a Treadmill in Kingstown' (McDonald, 1996: 320).

19 In 1872 the wearing of a mask in any street was made a petty offence in St Vincent. This Act was a widely ignored piece of legislation around carnival time on the island. An attempt to enforce this legislation in February 1879 led to urban rioting in Kingstown. The confrontation resulted in a police retreat from a mob, the loss of control of Kingstown for many hours and the dispatch of the warship HMS *Blanche* from Barbados to help quell the riot. Eventually, nine masqueraders were identified by the police as rioters, two appeared in a police court, and four were arrested and sentenced for assault.

3

Civilisation and wilderness: the St Vincent and the Grenadines context

There is a longstanding debate among analysts of the Caribbean about the notion of 'civilisation' and its meaning for the region. In the Caribbean, civilisation, work and language have been linked, admittedly in different ways and with different priorities, from colonial-through-postcolonial analyses from Anthony Trollope to George Lamming. Ian Strachan's *Paradise and Plantation* offers a rehearsal of the contradictory European metropolitan notions of civilisation and how they were visited on the Caribbean. He points out that work, however brutally organised, was equated with order and civilisation. He analyses in considerable detail the contradictory links, explored by Thomas Carlyle, Anthony Trollope and James Anthony Froude, among them the presumed laziness of slaves (embodying the 'wild': nature, chaos and that which needed to be tamed); the planters' and intellectuals' fear of the land returning to bush; and, in contrast, a growing lyricism in response to the beauty of the environment in its wild state.

At a practical level, the colonial authorities in St Vincent were anxious to improve the society and protect it from contamination by wild nature.[1] As historian Richard Drayton has shown, colonial government in the Caribbean has long been concerned with 'nature's government'. He points out, for example, that in 1765 St Vincent's Botanical Garden was the first of many overseas scientific gardens to function as a laboratory for cross-pollination experiments and was part of the perceived role of the colonial State as 'improver'. He observes: 'The rational use of Nature replaced piety as the foundation of imperial Providence, government became the Demiurge, and universal progress, measured by material abundance, its promised land' (Drayton, 2000: 80).

In colonial consciousness, this necessary ordering not only included flora and fauna but also encompassed, firstly, the Kalina and Garifuna populations who opposed imperial intrusion, and later, the enslaved and freed population of African origin. In his post Brigands' War euphoria after the British routed the Garifuna, for example, Charles Shepherd, chronicling the fighting, describes the Kalina as 'children of nature', and refers to the Garifuna at times as 'sanguinary monsters' and at others as a 'doubly savage race' (Shepherd, 1831: 65, 22).

In his journal John Anderson presents in a stark manner the dilemma, as he saw it, of the post-slavery relationship between civilisation and wilderness in St Vincent. A well-read scholar of his day, Anderson asks bluntly: can civilisation overcome the wilds of St Vincent? It is in his view a dilemma that is highly skewed against St Vincent with its mass of black population. He is in no doubt that St Vincent's black population is characterised by laziness, deceit and cunning. Nature, he declares, is the island's main provider: 'Nature has done everything for this beautiful isle, he – [man] nothing' (McDonald, 2001: 153). However, intellectually, Anderson recognises that he is part of what was known at the time as 'the Great Experiment', which posed the question: can the black population learn to labour voluntarily? In his journal he acknowledges, however reluctantly, that the mass of the population's attendance at church and their efforts to turn out in their best finery are early indications that the civilisation process has begun. However, he opines that civilisation faces insurmountable odds in favour of the wild, particularly in the form of inadequacy of labour and the poverty of language. Using St Vincent as his example, he suggests that it may take three generations more for the West Indies to 'possess' an 'enlightened and industrious peasantry' (McDonald, 2001: 118).

The concerns that civilisation might be halted, or even backslide, continued to be echoed by the colonial administration well into the nineteenth century. For example, in the late 1880s a major preoccupation in implementing the anglophone Caribbean's first land settlement scheme in St Vincent was a fear of labour regressing into 'African livelihood patterns' if settlement programmes were unsupervised. As Bonham Richardson points out: 'It was, of course, fear that was decades old, reinforced by contemporary discussions of releasing the region's black labour force from its subservient plantation existence' (Richardson, 1997: 220).

The change from a slave-based to an emancipated society did not change the underlying assumptions of white superiority among the colonial and planter elite. In contrast there was among the oppressed a keen awareness of the need to attain freedom and full participation in a society structured along class and colour lines. These contrasting perspectives could only result in periodic direct opposition and violent clashes when 'rights' and freedoms were seen to be challenged or impeded. As mentioned above, throughout each decade of the nineteenth and well into the twentieth century in St Vincent, there were riots or protests in which race or colour played a prominent part as a spur to conscious opposition when these rights were understood to be denied. From the white elite perspective these challenges were perceived as a weak character trait, a form of illogical behaviour characterised by the notion of the 'excitability' of the black masses. Whenever direct physical conflict threatened, the term 'excitable' – with its euphemistic assumption of a lack of self control leading to violence, that is 'wildness' – was a common feature of nineteenth-century colonial office reports on black and coloured crowd behaviour in Kingstown, and determined the actions to be taken for its suppression. One island administrator, while discussing the threat of the withdrawal of a number of eastern Caribbean island military garrisons, explained its manifestation in the following way: 'Everyone acquainted with the West Indies must admit that the negroes are highly excitable, and that in any disturbance the women are among the most prominent rioters.'[2] The tactic often used by the colonial elite in response was to delay negotiation to allow passions to cool before the local colonial office representatives met with protesters. In the face of the island's many riots throughout the nineteenth and into the twentieth century, it is clear that Kingstown was for the elite a place of only partial civilisation, where the 'wild' could also be encountered. In other words, a frontier.

By the turn of the twentieth century the notion of colonial civilisation that was on offer in St Vincent became more prosaic, associated with the spread of modern public medicine and education. From 1700 to 1850, the West Indies was commonly described as 'the cradle of fever', where it was not unusual for visitors to fall ill before they became 'acclimatised' or 'seasoned', and St Vincent was no exception. For many years fever had exacted a deadly toll on troops stationed in the islands. Between the years 1817 and 1836, for example, mortality rates for troops stationed on St Vincent were 11.2 per 1,000, caused by a variety of fevers (Boyce, 1910: 9). Island ports were described in Rubert Boyce's report as 'overcrowded, drainless, foul smelling collection[s] of huts, amongst the inhabitants of which fever was always present'. In addition, in St Vincent, smallpox, leprosy, tetanus and *mal rouge* were common (Boyce, 1910: 6).

In 1910, in the wake of the discovery of the yellow-fever-carrying mosquito, Boyce reported on the outcome of an active campaign of fever eradication in the region as nothing less than a civilising achievement. He asked: 'Why have malaria, yellow fever, cholera, and many other pestilences decreased or died out in the West Indies? The answer is: Civilisation with its attendant reforms, among which stand out education and hygiene: these have produced the beneficial changes' (Boyce, 1910: 34).

In the twentieth century, 'civilisation' became part of the ideology of Caribbean nation-building. For example, with the aspiration to promote a regional understanding of the term, undergraduate courses, to this day, are regularly taught on 'Caribbean civilisation' at all the main sites of the University of the West Indies.[3] The recommended texts in the manuals focus attention on issues of type and categorisation of 'civilisation'.[4]

St Vincent's postcolonial political leadership has not been immune to this desire to capture a notion of civilisation and to offer an interpretation of the term, albeit in the form of improving nature. Ralph

Gonsalves, the country's Prime Minister at the start of the twenty-first century and an outspoken promoter of 'Caribbean civilisation', has taken a more direct approach, presenting it as a form of national collective solidarity. He suggests: 'The true measure of our civilization is not in the individual efforts of our distinguished persons but in the community and solidarity of the people as a whole in the process of nation-building' (Gonsalves, 2001: 34).[5]

The notion of civilisation in the Caribbean, and specifically in the Vincentian context, has had a long and tortuous life. The more recent, postcolonial understandings of civilisation appear to have distanced themselves from the notion of the 'wild', consciously or otherwise ignoring the fact that they remain in an unspoken dialectical relationship with it. However overlooked or implicit, wildernesses are not difficult to locate. For the modern Caribbean state, as I have suggested elsewhere, the contemporary wilderness includes substantial acreage of land where illegal drugs are grown, or sea and air routes through which illegal substances are navigated. In the urban context it is found in places ineffectively policed by the State: for example areas with high crime rates, illegal drug associations and illegal shootings (even though police stations may be located in these areas). When these 'wild' areas are policed it is predominantly with the intention to subdue; the role of the police is not dissimilar to that of the pre-emancipation (white) citizens' militia (Nanton, 2004).

The important point here is that whether the analysis focuses on frontier, civilisation or wilderness it is apparent that the use of each of these terms has shifted conveniently, perhaps to convey a different emphasis or meaning at different times in the region's history. But the notion of the frontier, whether or not recognised as the locus for negotiating equilibrium between civilisation and the wild, remains very much alive. How might the frontier be located in early-twenty-first century St Vincent? The following section first discusses the waning of the frontier. Chapter 4 provides four examples of its resilience in what is now the island state of St Vincent and the Grenadines. Three examples are of frontier resilience by individuals, while the fourth is an illustration of wilderness as a frontier remnant.

The waning frontier

In 1891 the British imperial Government decided that St Vincent, which they considered more remote than Grenada, remained a sufficiently distant place to which they should expel King JaJa of Opobo, the palm oil middle-man trader who threatened their West African palm oil trade. However, despite this colonial acceptance of St Vincent's remoteness, Kingstown modernised slowly during the nineteenth century. And with this modernity, signs of frontier wilderness dissipated to some extent. Indications of this slowly growing modernity included the building of a local police barracks (started in 1873 and completed in 1875) – a building that also housed treasury and customs and excise departments. A colonial hospital was built in 1878 and the provision of street lighting for a few central streets was begun in 1891. In 1907 the island's Carnegie-donated public library in Kingstown was opened (Archer, 1932). In the late twentieth century, with increasing political autonomy and the achievement of political independence in 1979, the island saw itself no longer as a periphery or, to use colonial parlance, a 'minor colony', and by the end of the twentieth century the term 'city' began to be used to describe the capital. Other major features of modernisation included land reclamation by dredging along the Kingstown harbour in the 1960s and, to the east of the town, the construction of a deep-water harbour; a central bus station and new markets for fish, meat and vegetables were provided by donor countries during the tenure of James 'Son' Mitchell as Prime Minister.[6]

Kingstown, the capital and frontier town, continues to offer a mixture of modernity and dilapidation. Make an imaginative leap to twenty-first-century Kingstown and you quickly discover a hot and hard urban space with business or party politics on its mind. There has been a gradual exodus of residents from the town centre, first to Edinboro to the east of the capital in the late nineteenth century, followed by housing developments in the surrounding hills of Montrose to the north- east, and Cane Garden to the west of Kingstown, all former plantation lands. Montrose, now a suburb of Kingstown, was acquired by the State to house public servants. Cane Garden was sold to private buyers in lots of varying sizes.

The city centre is dominated by a covered vegetable market and the House of Assembly. From off shore the backdrop of mountains and green hills is dotted with houses, but very few green areas soften the town centre's poorly maintained and foot-buckling cobblestones, asphalt and concrete. Instead, there are signs of attempts to banish nature from the town. Photographs from the 1930s show a town with trees lining the front of the bay as well as on the outskirts of the town to the east known as the 'Frenches'. They were all cut down. Vivian Child, a Vincentian historian, suggests that this was on the advice of the local health inspector who, she notes, 'seems to have imbued a whole gener- ation with a mistrust of trees near habitations … for "Health" reasons' (Child, 2004: 30). The cobble-stones in the town centre are now frayed, leaving gaps and divots between the stones. Main roads are clogged with cars either parked or searching for parking spaces, at rush hour forming long queues to enter or leave the capital.[7] Along the centre of the capital's main roads men push hand-made wooden barrows six to seven feet long at walking pace to and from the port or supermarket. They transport for their customers weekly shopping, coconuts, sacks of potatoes or gas canisters. Cars give them priority as they walk in the road. A mid-twentieth-century experiment in establishing town centre traffic lights failed. At first they worked intermittently, then not at all. They stand ignored and rusting on road sides or suspended above the main roads.

Though the purpose-built covered market hosts around 350 ven- dors, another 150 or so prefer to take their chances outside (the rates are cheaper, collectors easier to avoid). Some erect temporary biv- ouacs of canvas that cover as much ground as the vegetable market, or sit in the shade of every permanent overhang. They display on camp beds or rough wood or plastic tables their small-scale items for sale: heaps of fruit, ground provisions, braziers, sports trainers, telephone cards and boot-legged DVDs and CDs. A few self-styled preachers with clanging bell, Bible, tambourine or squeaking microphone stand at intersections and shout warnings of hell fire or extol the benefits of repentance. The wide drains of the main streets are open. It is not difficult to spot a rat or two scuttling along the shaded side of these drains.

Notes

1 For Valentine Morris's eighteenth-century ideas about how to 'civilise' the Garifuna (that is, impressing them by building forts, trading with them offering what he called 'baubles', and sending a few Garifuna chiefs to London to show the might of the British navy), see Waters (1964), 39–40, and Fabel (2000), 202–203.
2 Francis Hincks to Henry Pelham, Duke of Newcastle, Public Record Office, London, Colonial Office military confidential report no. 49, 7 September 1861.
3 I know of no comparable course on the 'Caribbean wild'.
4 See for example the worksheets *Journeying after Arrival*, University of the West Indies, Cave Hill Campus, Barbados.
5 His government strategies to implement 'civilisation', along with those of his predecessor, Sir James 'Son' Mitchell, are discussed in the context of their autobiographies in Chapter 5.
6 For a full personal statement of Mitchell's 'civilising' achievements during his three terms of office in the role of Prime Minister see Mitchell (2006).
7 There certainly exists an official belief that the wilderness has been banished from twenty-first-century Kingstown. For example, an official sign at Kingstown's ferry terminal, where boats between Kingstown and various Grenadine islands dock, proclaims: 'Welcome to Kingstown, you are entering a hub of commercial activities.'

4

Frontier retentions

Managing (and not managing) 'wild' frontier remnants: the St Vincent Grenadines

In this chapter I wish to tease out the different, more contemporary meanings of the frontier in the southern extreme of the collective thirty-two-island state of SVG. To the south of the St Vincent main island lie the Grenadines. They stretch over some 60.4 km (37.5 mi) and have a combined area of 45 km² (17.4 mi²). Roughly two-thirds of these islets belong to SVG and the rest to Grenada. Seven of the larger St Vincent Grenadine islands have permanent inhabitants. They include Bequia, Mustique, Canouan, Mayreau, Palm Island, Petit St Vincent and Union Island. The remaining islets comprise uninhabited smaller rock formations of various sizes and shapes above the water line. What frontier issues might a small sovereign state with such a porous and variegated southern boundary (peripheries of a periphery) experience?

Before 1792, concessions to settle the Grenadines were given to colonisers by both French and British governors. Most of the islands that were large enough to support a small population became associated with single landowning families: for example the St Hillaires of Mayreau, the Snagg family of Canouan, and, in the twentieth century, the Eustace family of Mustique and the Tobago Cays. They operated simple social systems that tied the populations, of no more than a few hundred on each populated island, to the land through sharecropping, keeping of animals and fishing. In the twentieth century a small proportion of the men, many of whom were good sailors, obtained half-yearly employment working as seamen on ocean-going bulk transport ships registered in Liberia or Panama.

Until the late twentieth century neglect and degradation have been the historical experiences of each tiny populated Grenadine island. This neglect took the form of a lack of basic amenities as a result of mainland uninterest from successive Government administrations, both colonial and postcolonial. The island of Canouan illustrates the common experience of neglect and resource shortages. Located near the middle of the chain of the Grenadines, Canouan comprises a mere 1,832 acres (741 ha). In a period of about 100 years – that is, until 1986 – the island's population crept up only to 800 people. Before 1955 there was no police station, and although it had a small fee-paying primary school dating from 1897, the first government school was opened in 1928. A medical doctor and dentist might visit monthly, depending on weather conditions. The first political elections were superficial events that offered ineffective representation. The first representative for the Grenadines region never visited the island. Residents remember that the next representative couldn't be bothered to visit, even when in 1958 Hurricane Janet hit the island destroying most of the buildings. With regular droughts from 1930, drinking water had to be imported each dry season for fifty years. In the early 1990s the island remained without so basic an amenity as electricity. One past Prime Minister, Sir James F. Mitchell, a descendant of a Canouan islander, summarised the longstanding plight of the Grenadines through the experience of this island. He described Canouan as 'a remote island, with a small population encircled by hostile winds and currents, lacking both strategic importance, and voting power, [that] did not consequentially, at any historical point in time draw the attention of the various administrations – who remained indifferent to its infrastructural and other developmental needs' (Mitchell, 1996: 194).

Neglect has reinforced strong island loyalties and led to occasional attempts at secession. The most recent was in 1979, when a small group in Union Island, SVG's most southern dependency, led by Lennox

'Bumber' Charles, failed in an attempt by military arms to separate that island from the then fledgling State of SVG.[1]

This historic frontier status, characterised by central Government indifference and neglect, has, in the past twenty or so years, changed dramatically. The reason is the lure of the 'exotic wild' for the wealthy yachting tourist or foreign homeowner. Bequia has established an international reputation as a destination for yachting enthusiasts. In 1958, for a sum of GBP45,000, Mustique was acquired on a long lease by Colin Tennant. By 1993, the Mustique Company had built seventy-five foreign exclusive homes and another twenty-five people had bought development lots (Vaughn, 1994: 28). In 1995 two-thirds of Canouan was leased to the Italian-Swiss developer Antonio Saladino, who headed the company Canouan Resorts Development Ltd (CRD) (Lewis, 2010). The modern frontier appeal these atolls hold is their remoteness. Fed by year-round warm breeze, sunshine and substantial foreign capital expenditure, these features conspire to turn frontier remoteness into frontier exclusivity and exoticism.

Firstly, for the newly arrived entrepreneur who plans to invest in the island there is the Crusoe act of 'discovery' and a romantic Crusoe experience. The author of a thick coffee-table picture book about Mustique, the foreword of which claims 'This book is about fantasy realized' (Vaughn, 1994: n.p.), describes a first experience of the then undeveloped Palm Island in the following way: 'It was heaven at first … To be alone on the island with no development … We lived a Robinson Crusoe life there. We had nothing, but we had ourselves, and the nicest thing in the world is to own nothing' (Vaughn, 1994: 5). Saladino, the main expatriate entrepreneur in Canouan, recounted to me his Canouan Crusoe experience when he first stumbled across that island:

> The discovery of the island of Canouan was as a result of sailing with friends on a motor yacht and visiting most of the Grenadine islands … we saw this unknown, beautiful, lush land and having sailed around, were astounded by the number of great beaches. The combination of lush and strong colours of the vegetation with the pure turquoise of the waters was

very reminiscent of the island of Sardinia and its outer islands. The obvious question was why no developer had ventured there.[2]

These tourism developers offer their clients the frontier experience of an exclusive and romanticised relationship with nature. The author of *Mustique* suggests that: 'the best thing about Mustique is that after 35 years of development, the construction of seventy-five houses, and the passage of thousands of visitors, one can still make solitary music on Mustique from the rhythm of the beetles' (Vaughn, 1994: n.p.).

Wealthy developers have now put substantial amounts of money for tourism development into at least five tiny SVG island developments. In return they usually obtain a wide range of taxation and other lucrative privileges for their investments. This is, of course, all part of the frontier financial process.[3] But how do islanders, from St Vincent and Canouan respectively, experience the frontier process? In 1990 CRD acquired 1,200 acres (485.6 ha) – around two-thirds of Canouan – on a long lease from the Government of SVG. It since acquired another 78 acres (31.6 ha) from the State's United Labour Party Government. The company spent over $200 million on infrastructure – roads, electricity, water desalination plants, a health clinic – and rebuilt the local police station. It has built a new airport; repaired hurricane destruction damage promptly; and with business tourism partners built a hotel, a golf course, a casino and holiday villas for sale. Foreign partner developers come and go (they have included Donald Trump, the hotel chain Raffles and most recently the Irish developer Dermot Desmond). The most recent strategy appears now to be similar to that pursued in Mustique, essentially constructing homes for exclusive foreign home ownership. Before arriving at this goal the frontier living experience of islanders was somewhat different.

As recently as the 1980s, local Canouan households were required to be self-sufficient. They supported themselves on their own produce: salt collection, but mainly by fishing and small-scale agriculture: growing peas, corn and cassava. Local residents stored their harvests and sold the produce after they replanted. There was local fishing for men and whelk collection on the rocks around the coast for women. In the absence of refrigeration, preserving fish by salting for domestic use or sale – a process locally known as 'corning' – was widespread and long established. Sailors also worked on merchant shipping for half-year periods.

Since the exclusive tourism developments on the island, many Canouan people have restructured their way of life. In a period of about fifteen years the shift has been from centuries of almost subsistence living to servicing international tourism. From the company's point of view the rate of this process has been hampered by an inherited low standard of education and an economy traditionally based on farming and fishing. The islanders appreciate the employment and have expressed surprise at the company's willingness to support individuals in difficult circumstances. They can see the tangible changes to their living conditions – more regular health care, opportunities for house ownership and for educating their children to secondary school level, as well as the opportunity to obtain computing and other technical skills, all of which were in short supply when they were younger.

However, the process of change has not been problem-free. Periodic protests reflect islanders' feelings of exclusion from what many regarded as their birthright. In the early stages of hotel development in the 1990s the local population protested at the desecration of grave sites while the resort was being built. I spoke with one elderly lady who led the protest and who described to me her concerns:

Tan-tan's testament

I lay down in the road, mister gentleman. As God is my witness. I lay right down in that road. I tell them run your machine, your tractor and your bulldozer over me if you want. But it wrong. It wrong, wrong, wrong what they do and I don't care who I tell. Hope is my family name. We live in this island generation upon generation. From the time they bring my great, great gran-pappy out of Guinea. My naval string bury under a tree on Yambou land. All my family bury in Massa Sam cemetery. Gran-Pappy, Gran-Ma, Auntie Leticia, my Cedric, all of them. That company just reach. They machines mash down every living piece of cemetery, not a head stone, a flowers pot, not one mark in the earth remain mister gentleman. It was a Saturday morning, ten-thirty. Sun hot as hell. We and all the village go up to the company gate. We shouting and we holler 'Desecration! Destruction! Look me here, take me now! Bring all your guard, all your gun, all your dog them, we not moving.'

Look this picture. Cedric, my Cedric. He a sharp man, eh? Rest he soul. It take out in High Wycombe, England. He come back to dead and bury here in Massa Sam cemetery. I make two daughters for he and they bury there too. We was friending long before he go to England.

But mister gentleman the company people know it was wrong what they do. Them know it. Tree weeks after they move all we old galvanise, old drum, old car tyre, rock stone that we put in the road, two white people come to my gate early of an evening calling out 'Tan-tan, Tan-tan'. I don't know how they know my name so. I look out the door and is one manager that I recognise and a woman with he. I never see she before. She dress nice nice, not like me in this old frock.

Hear them: 'We want to talk with you, Tan-tan.'

I say is jail for me now. But I don't care, they does do what they want anyhow.

So I says to them: 'Who send you to me? If the company send you I have nothing to say.'

Hear them: 'Nobody send us. We just want to talk.'

So I tell them: 'The door open, you could come in if you want.'

Just as you and me sit down on this step here they come and sit down. Well, they come to say they sorry. They did not know that the graveyard mean so much to the village. They ask me if I want anything. Well, mister gentleman what me going to do? I tell them I don't want nothing. I tell them is not to me they must say sorry. Is they conscience and is a power greater than me they will have to reckon with. So we sit and we talk. The lady show me picture of she family. I show she the same picture of my Cedric that I show you. When they leave me they say them going put things right. I look them straight in the eye but I not saying nothing. My mouth get me in trouble already.

But I think to myself how they could do that? When you bury, you rest with you own.

I don't know where Cedric remains gone now. When I dead how I going lie next to he? It all done and mash up. When my time come, you might as well throw my remains in the sea.

In 1999 an instruction handbook circulated by CRD on cleanliness and deportment won few friends among the resort employees. Islanders have been frustrated by low-grade levels of employment and the experience of exclusive tourism. The latter involves building and maintaining resort buildings, villas and beach facilities in which they are primarily welcome for their menial labour. To quote Mitchell's observation about the islanders' experience of this form of frontier development, 'The problem is that the people of Canouan don't feel they belong in their own country' (Mitchell, 1989). This sense of ostracism is reinforced by the many Vincentians (around 400) from the main island who regularly seek employment in Canouan. One former senior manager at the resort was of the opinion that relations between the local population and other Vincentians working on the island were a major source of intra-state tensions – the (main island) Vincentian employees felt exploited by Canouan islanders, who they claim rack up rates for poor-quality accommodation. Canouan islanders resent what they see as little respect for their island and the loss of their potential jobs. In addition, the local working population is excluded from resort facilities outside work hours, and with few if any amenities for their use there has been a severe problem of drunkenness in the island's one local village at weekends. With predominantly white guests and predominantly black employees, not surprisingly, the protests also took on a racialised form in the local telling.[4] In the 1999/2000 tourist season some of these early issues spilled over into a protest involving a week-long attempted blockade of the resort, arrests, rock-throwing incidents, demonstrations against CRD and public meetings with Government officials. The conflict also brought into the open the feeling that official priorities were not in the interests of the populations of the islands.[5]

Other forms of frontier retention

In other ways St Vincent society continues to betray enduring and distinguishing marks of its frontier experience. These marks, both at the collective and individual level, though often ignored, are to be found as much in the island's contemporary revisionist history as in traces of individual lifestyles.

Revisionist history

One location of the modern frontier is in the mythic notion of the frontier hero. I use the notion of a 'frontier hero myth' here as a form of inverted colonial moral landscape in which wilderness/civilisation and black/white racial borders are among the most basic (Slotkin, 1973). The central point here is that in the constructed collective memory of emancipation and political independence, black figures are required to be seen to be exercising autonomy and power, and black agency and defiance are important for the imagining of freedom. This process is not new but it has taken increasingly official form. Thus, in 2002 the Government of SVG declared Chatoyer, Chief of the Caribs, St Vincent's first national hero. Chatoyer was represented as the leader of a horde of 'sanguinary monsters' by the nineteenth-century colonial historian Charles Shepherd. Chatoyer has been exonerated by revisionist history.[6] Originally depicted also as part of the 'wild' by white settlers, and surviving at the conflicted border between the 'wild' and 'civilisation', Chatoyer's life history offers all the elements of a modern mythic frontier hero. He took up arms against encroachment; organised and led a resistance struggle; died in battle in disputed circumstances; and has been resurrected in the twenty-first century, no longer a villain but now a heroic figure.[7] One location in which frontier heroism resides, ideologically, is in the myth of nation-building. The role of the myth-hero is central to this process, and heroes are the handmaiden to freedom. It stems from a history that fails to recognise that moments of historical transformation are often ambiguous. It offers a perspective that for the most part presents history as a continuum, and frontier heroism as a predominantly male activity. Nationalist history, then, requires a purpose and a direction.[8] Mythic frontier heroes are predominantly male. What, one may legitimately ask, has this to do with St Vincent as a representative of the modern frontier?

The answer is that the nation state has to look for frontier heroes not only in early history but in more modern history as well. In 1979, the year that SVG became politically independent, Rupert John published a volume that described the lives of twenty-two Vincentians with an emphasis on 'the contributions they made during the early years of the twentieth century to the political, economic, social or cultural development of their native land' (John, 2009: n.p.). Entitled *Pioneers in Nation-Building in a Caribbean Mini-State*, the volume drew on conventional frontier notions of individuals from various professional backgrounds – education, press, business, agriculture – who fought against great odds and worked tirelessly to improve nature (and thus by implication to banish the 'wild') in their various disciplines. At the same time these chosen 'pioneers' exhibited a third traditional mythic frontier characteristic: all twenty-two of the lives celebrated were male. The frontier theme was revived in 2012 when a two-volume collection of essays was published offering brief biographies of another thirty-three individuals from later in the twentieth century. The collection was edited by Baldwin King and Cheryl Phills King. In this more recent collection the group of subjects are no longer described as 'pioneers', but 'trailblazers'. For the most part, the same themes of endurance and achievement against great odds are celebrated. The preface to Volume II of this collection states that 'by dint of intellect, hard work and perseverance, [they] have succeeded in moving the beautiful island of St Vincent and the Grenadines … a little further along, either directly or indirectly' (King and King, 2011: 7). Male dominance also remained a feature, with only seven of the thirty-three lives celebrated in the collection being female. In this way, the revisionist trend in nationalist history has managed to keep the frontier very much alive.

At the individual level, Gordon Lewis has drawn attention to the rawness of frontier lifestyles. He offers the particular example of log-wood cutters who settled in the Campeachy and Honduras areas of the Yucatan peninsula from the mid-seventeenth century onward. His description captures some of the elements that inform the notion of the individual on the frontier: 'primitive institutional organisation; a violent distrust of authority, especially any authority to do with govern-ment; a masterful grasp of material things – combined with acuteness and acquisitive instincts; a great dislike for anything philosophical; a genius for ready action' (Lewis, 1968: 82). Though these characteristics are specific to the location and date back hundreds of years, they are also characteristic of frontier lives in general. While not all remain alive at the individual level in twenty-first-century St Vincent, a number can be shown to exist in a modernised form.

The vignettes below offer an eclectic collection of four contemporary scenarios that capture the vibrancy of the modern frontier in SVG. The first describes the experience of attending a 'dame school' in Kingstown in the 1950s; the next presents the frontier in the context of innovations applied by a medical practitioner, a self styled 'isolated surgeon'; and third, the surviving inland frontier is represented through the work of an individual lumber cutter, or woodsman. The final example describes the politics of managing a frontier resource.

Modern frontier retentions

The dame school teacher

In the 1950s dame schools in St Vincent operated alongside Church-based schooling and public Government-funded schools on the island. They were home-based institutions run by one or two women, often a spinster on her own or perhaps with a sister. I know of no formal record or study of the history or nature of dame schools in the Caribbean context and certainly not in St Vincent. The following observations, therefore, are based on the author's personal recollection of attending such a school for varying lengths of time in St Vincent during this period. This particular school was owned and run by Miss Nelcia John and located in a two-storey house near the centre of Kingstown. At that time there were at least three existing dame schools operating in Kingstown, one of which was operated by Miss Nelcia's sisters in 'Bottom Town', at the western end of the town. At Miss Nelcia's, one bedroom was hired out to a secondary school student from outside Kingstown attending the island's elite grammar school. The remaining bedrooms, living room and, if demand was sufficiently high, out-house area, were converted each morning into classrooms and dismantled and returned to their traditional home use after school each afternoon. For make-shift desks Miss John combined the use of her household furniture along with a few long wooden trellis tables and benches, depending on the number of children attending. These were also set up and dismantled each day as the children's first and last task. Cash payment was made each term for each child attending the school. In St Vincent, the dame school was notorious for its much stricter regimen and closer supervision than the Government or Church schools. Some fifteen to twenty children of various primary school ages attended the school at this time. Parents would enrol their primary school children if they could afford the fee and if they considered their child or children to be failing to achieve in the larger Government or Church schools.

Miss John offered a form of private elementary education that paid attention to reading, writing – especially cursive practice – arithmetic and Bible study. She extended this curriculum to include English grammar, in particular parts of speech and parsing of sentences. The discipline was notoriously strict – one reason that parents choose her school – and substantial amounts of rote learning and homework completion were required. The rote learning and memory-based tests were often linked to verses of the Bible, poems and popular speeches from certain of Shakespeare's plays.

The dame school represented a long-established female frontier activity that in many countries dated back to the eighteenth century.

The school mimicked the larger State or Church-based schools, for example in its method of rote learning and discipline. However, the dame school offered the individual female teacher a means to make an independent living, an opportunity often restricted for women in frontier societies. Other frontier elements were that an improvised form of schooling reflected the violence of the frontier on a small scale, with children regularly beaten for small misdemeanours in their set lesson tasks. At times, when they were closely supervised, younger children would shake with fear. Of course, at this time violence also applied in other schools; however, the greater intimacy of the dame school and the easier oversight of its small group made for a more intense experience of frontier education.

The 'isolated' surgeon

The life work of one general surgeon, who saved countless lives through his improvisational methods, offers another example of modern frontier life in St Vincent. Born in 1927, when general surgeon Cecil Cyrus retired from practice in 2001 his career in the field of medicine had spanned thirty-nine years. He became a legend among medical practitioners in the Caribbean and internationally. During his professional life he was elected a fellow of the American College of Surgeons in 1980, and in 1990 he was awarded the Master of Surgery degree for his self-published *A Clinical and Pathological Atlas: The Records of a Surgeon in St Vincent, the West Indies.* The book illustrates and discusses many of the conditions that he attended during his decades of practice. In the world of medicine he was known before his retirement as 'the isolated surgeon of St Vincent'. He coined the phrase himself, using it in over forty medical papers presented to his peers.

After Cyrus qualified in Britain in 1957 he returned to work in St Vincent out of a sense of responsibility to his society. For a time he was employed in the public service but found the terms and conditions unacceptable, and after a variety of disagreements with the island's official health service, he established his own clinic and eventually a small hospital. He was known especially for his inventiveness associated with the surgical implements that he employed when treating patients. In May 2002 he opened a small museum of his life and his work in St Vincent, which has since closed. When I visited it and interviewed him in 2006, he kept in one corner what he called his favourite implements, those with which he had had to improvise in his surgical practice. They included screwdrivers of various sizes, with metal instead of wooden handles (for easier sterilisation); electric drills and home-made lead weights for traction – in his day the officially available sandbags leaked; and his favourite invention – three hollow metal objects, each roughly the size of a wine cork, with a serrated outer edge. These were home-made 'trephines' for burr holes, used as attachments to the electric drill, for freeing blood trapped in the brain. They were constructed by a local metal-work teacher for his use. He estimated that he had used some thirty-six locally made improvised instruments to save or restore countless lives. His observation on the circumstances with which he had to contend in St Vincent speaks directly to the frontier: 'We are a long suffering people. Here we survive often against all odds' (Nanton, 2006: 55).

The frontier activities described here indicate the survival of characteristics Lewis indicated in connection with the frontier logwood cutters. The disenchantment with and distrust of officialdom, capacity for innovation and a genius for ready action each have a role in the experience and attitude of the isolated surgeon in St Vincent.

The woodcutter

Lawrence Guy is a retired woodcutter. He was born in 1922 in Marriaqua Valley of St Vincent and attended Marriaqua Government School. By age eleven he was learning carpentry, joinery and masonry from his father. By 1933 he had become interested in farming and entered Glenn Community School to study agriculture, but was pulled between the two callings. He completed his secondary schooling in 1935, achieving his school certificate. From this time his very mobile lifestyle began. He migrated twice to Aruba but returned to St Vincent after relatively short stays and took up farming, first by leasing land and eventually being employed as a senior buyer, estate manager and skilled worker on relatively large estates in the Leeward valley (Queensbury and Penniston), owned by members of the Punnett family. Guy's skill range is diverse. He became both a trusted estate employee and an independent woodcutter who practised various forms of carpentry.

This brief sketch does little justice to Lawrence Guy's diverse and full life. I present these summary points to capture a frontier lifestyle that has to be understood in the context of the particular geography of the island. It is a rural geography in which those living in the two main geographical areas of the island, Leeward and Windward, are separated by mountains and relatively sealed off from one another. Communication has of course improved, with Kingstown, Leeward's hub, linked to Windward by the coastal road. However, while there are plans afoot, there is as yet no joining highway across either the centre or north of the island. As Queensbury resident and local commentator Mike Kirkwood has pointed out, although Guy has lived almost continuously in the Leeward Buccament Valley since his twenties, he remains a Leeward outsider. How is this possible in a small island of less than 389 km² (150 mi²)? Kirkwood notes: 'St Vincent is bifurcated into two zones with very different coastlines, sea conditions and topographical features on either side of a central southeast–northwest tending ridge system.' There are a few paths but they are known to a handful of people who undertake to travel them regularly and they at times live for weeks in the dense undergrowth to earn a living. Guy is an outsider to Leeward people but one who knows well the mountain routes and how to move between these relatively hermetically sealed regions of the island. Kirkwood's notes and in-depth interviews with Lawrence Guy, on which he has allowed me to draw, capture the essence of Guy's Vincentian frontiersman existence. For example, he offers the following word picture of Lawrence Guy the frontiersman: 'Journeying constantly between high Windward and deep Leeward, Guy, with his nine foot saw braced in bamboo covers and slung over his shoulder, is indeed a moving spirit.'[9]

The lifestyle and personal background of Guy summarised here are not unique, and although his is a declining lifestyle it is not in danger of disappearing altogether. In St Vincent such frontierspeople include other woodcutters, hunters, cray-fishermen, mountain farmers and, more recently, ganja growers. As Kirkwood has observed, for such people 'mobility across the ridges (although central they are folded and discontinuous, enclosing hundreds of ravines ("gutters") and inland valleys) is a key to livelihood. Following this life meant spending weeks at a time in the rain forest.'[10]

Managing frontier resources

The final illustration of the contemporary SVG frontier that I will examine is the protest that erupted in 2003 that was critical of the management proposals for a portion of the St Vincent Grenadines called the Tobago Cays. In 1997 the Tobago Cays Marine Park (TCMP) was inaugurated. The TCMP comprises a total of 66 km^2 (25.5 mi^2) and encompasses nine islands of SVG. Four are uninhabited (Petit Bateau, Jamesby, Baradal and Petit Tabac); Mayreau contains a small population of almost 300 residents; and the TCMP area also includes the nearby tiny uninhabited outgrowths of Catholic Island, Jandal and Mayreau Beleine. A series of beaches, reefs and shallows surround the islands. The Cays form a natural water park with coral reefs and sea grass beds that support a variety of fish, sea turtles and sea birds. The islands contain beach vegetation, dry forests and iguanas.

In 1942 Mayreau and the Tobago Cays came into the possession of the Eustace family of SVG. In 1960 the Tobago Cays alone were sold to Nicholas Fuller, an American who was head of the Tobago Cays Holding Co. Ltd of Antigua. In 1999, after protracted negotiations, the then SVG Prime Minister, James Mitchell, secured their return to St Vincent ownership on condition that the Cays remain a conservation water park and that no commercial activity should be allowed in connection with the islands. The area increasingly needed regulating as the numbers of day-trip and yachting visitors increased. How was this process to be managed? From 1991 to 2002 at least four groups of plans had been drawn up for the management of the area but to little effect. In 2003 it was leaked that the SVG Government, led by Prime Minister Ralph Gonsalves, was negotiating with James Barrett, the American business manager of Palm Island Resort Limited, terms and conditions under which he would manage TCMP. Local opposition led by two organisations, the Mayreau Environmental Development Organisation and the Friends of the Tobago Cays, was galvanised against the arrangement. Political party opposition was also active against the proposed arrangement. The combined opposition disputed the terms of the negotiations, the conservation and environmental competence of the proposed management, and the personnel to be involved. It was argued that Barratt had no conservation experience and that his plans breached the initial terms of the return of the TCMP to local ownership, and it was considered an insult to local expertise that the management should be put in the hands of an outsider. A heated nine months' campaigning and debate followed. The issue was resolved when Barratt withdrew his proposal and the SVG Government was required to establish a public-based management committee for the park.

Mustique, Canouan and the Tobago Cays are frontier locations at the margins of the State. Various governments of SVG have negotiated formal agreements and terms of use of the islands with private tourism developers. The SVG Government has minority representation on the board of Mustique. It is approached periodically to intervene where there are confrontations with the local population. These interventions often come too little and too late. Canouan developers complain that they carry the responsibility of the local State. In the Tobago Cays the State misjudged local feeling about how to manage this element of the island frontier. Thus, beyond the essentially formal arrangements between Government and developer, these islands are locations where, as Veena Das and Deborah Poole suggest, 'the state project is always incomplete'

(Das and Poole, 2004: 8). Local parties are required for the most part to work out some form of agreement among themselves.

The Grenadine islands provide the opportunity for private developers to exploit the notion of the exotic frontier. Their substantial funds give them the freedom to construct for their clients romantic and exotic notions that promote the illusion that they exist in their own world. Their investments enable their clients to buy, for a limited time, a privileged, somewhat misleading closeness to nature.

In conclusion it would appear that frontier-based analysis has the advantage of providing a method of exploring landscape through a cultural and historical geography that pays attention to place, population and process. Today's context of environmental depredation has increasingly shifted the emphasis from exploitation and development to the need for the protection of wild nature. Rather than exhuming a limited notion of the frontier as a concern about borders, I am suggesting that the frontier in SVG has survived and indeed thrived. I have demonstrated this survival in the form of a number of individuals in the St Vincent context. At the same time it is apparent that a critical feature in studying the frontier now is the relationship that is worked out between the notion of the frontier and a remnant of 'wild nature'.

Far from being moribund, a long view of the frontier process in St Vincent suggests that it is possible to trace both individual and collective frontier continuities that have survived from earliest colonial times. At the individual level of the three case studies presented above there is a streak of determination that is highlighted through the lens of modern frontier. It is a determination that goes beyond mere survival and instead makes the best of the situation. It requires a fierce individualism, inventiveness and a determination to turn local circumstances, however rough, to one's advantage.

At the collective level the long history of the frontier experience is a more troubling one. The individualism that the frontier betrays in white planter absentee culture (essentially a neglect or contempt for public institutions of various sorts) has a number of parallels in the new black political class. It is demonstrated ultimately by a form of indifference to the public good. This may sound a harsh judgement on a Caribbean society that, like many others, has struggled to maintain public welfare programmes, education and all the trappings of institutions of the public good.[11] At the same time, if one looks under the surface of the society, as this chapter has sought to demonstrate, frontier continuities abound. In the eighteenth century tracts of St Vincent's land are auctioned off when the colonial State steps in. In the twentieth century, yes, at times, tracts of the St Vincent mainland are prohibited to foreign buyers and preserved for local use.[12] But large parts of St Vincent's Grenadines peripheries, long neglected by old and newer regimes, are also traded on long lease to wealthy private capital interests. The institutions that are established there ensure that the frontier experience in various forms remains a robust, albeit a modernised, one, tailored and even regulated for commercial consumption.

St Vincent's Garifuna and black 'wild' was regularly put down by the old (white) militia. The (black) police force or regiment is now expected to banish 'wild' ganja farmers or those in urban areas whose behaviour is similarly deemed to undermine this new and commercially acceptable version of 'wildness'.

Governments of every persuasion throughout SVG history continue to banish the wilderness by establishing 'civilising' institutions. To my earlier colonial examples of wilderness being banished might be added the St Vincent Botanical Gardens, Kingstown Grammar School and Girls' High School, newspapers, agricultural reforms and land settlement schemes of various periods, to name a few. Most of these institutions, now postcolonial, struggle to sustain themselves. The reason for this, I suggest, is that the frontier conditions that I describe are more deeply engrained in SVG history and social relations with itself and others than it is willing to admit.

Epilogue

While writing up my notes in a hotel bar in Canouan I was approached by a hotel cleaner, a Mrs Rock. She saw me writing and stopped to talk; our chat quickly became a desperate sales pitch.

Mrs Rock's pitch

You writing a book? I thought so. You see, it good to ask a question. You know the man from Barbados? It say on the radio he come from Barbados. He going to join with the owners of the hotel up there with the houses. I can't remember the man name. Anyway, I want to talk to he. I have a piece of land. I want to cut it and keep the bottom piece and sell him the top half. He could make a hotel there. I have family that he can employ. I can't remember the man name, though. I wonder how I could talk to he. He have one of them house up north. I recall his name now. He name Trump. If you see him tell him I have a piece of land for sale. My brother will live in the bottom piece and I will live there too when I retire. I am a Rock. I related to all them island family.

Notes

1 For discussions of this episode see Nanton (1983), 170.
2 From text of an email interview conducted with Antonio Saladino by Philip Nanton, July 2006.
3 For a summary of concessions negotiated by CRD in Canouan see Lewis (2010).
4 A letter to *Searchlight*, an SVG newspaper, written by one Samantha Smart (a possible pseudonym), claimed: 'The real truth is that the European elite in Canouan have no love for black people, have no appreciation of the beauty of Afro-Caribbean culture, no respect for Vincentian traditions and individuals. The real truth is that management does not want to see black bodies at the beach with white bodies lounging carelessly nearby. Black bodies will only be acceptable in the uniforms of servants: maids, bartenders, lawns men and concierges. Saladino did not come to Canouan because he loved the people but because he loved the property.' *Searchlight*, 9 February 2001, 11.
5 Renwick Rose, a regular columnist for *Searchlight*, observed at the time of the dispute: 'A psychology of mega projects has enveloped our politicians and bureaucratic elite. They consider infrastructural development to be more important than HUMAN development.' The result, he suggested, was: 'big bucks and big concessions to which we must all bow or be counted as "ungrateful".' *Searchlight*, 10 November 2000, 7.
6 For early revision of Chatoyer's history see Kirby and Martin (1986). For more recent revision see Fraser (2002). For a muddier view of Garifuna leadership during the Brigands' Wars see Fabel (2000), 193. Fabel gives prominence to the role of one Jean-Baptiste during the first Brigands' War (186).

7 In this context Richard Slotkin provides a useful definition of what he calls the 'myth-hero'. Slotkin states: 'a myth is a narrative which concentrates in a single, dramatised experience the whole history of a people in their land. The myth-hero embodies or defends the values of his culture in a struggle against the forces which threaten to destroy the people and lay waste the land' (Slotkin, 1973: 269).

8 An alternative, 'humanist' perspective on history – one that leans more towards illuminating rather than necessarily joining the fragments – is proposed for the Caribbean by Richard Drayton. He argues that because history has fault lines like any other discipline, these should be recognised and not glossed over – the inherent danger of nationalist history being that it shares much of the teleological style of its colonialist predecessor (Drayton, 2004: 16).

9 These quotations are part of an undated, extended series of interviews and observations conducted in Buccament, St Vincent with Lawrence Guy by Michael J. Kirkwood around 2006. I am grateful for access to them.

10 *Ibid.*

11 In 2008, the total population of SVG was estimated at approximately 120,000 inhabitants. Some 30.2 per cent of the SVG population was deemed to be poor, 2.9 per cent indigent, and 48.2 per cent of the population was estimated to be below the vulnerability (to poverty) line. Remittances accounted for 22.1 per cent of all household incomes (Kairi Consultants Ltd., 2008). In his presentation of the 2011 budget to the St Vincent House of Assembly the Prime Minister and Minister of Finance, Ralph Gonsalves, stated that SVG Government welfare benefits are directly paid to or on behalf of 6,000 people – of these 5,600 are on public assistance, and one-third are students of poor families. In 2010, SVG public debt was EC$1.23 billion: that is 63.6 per cent of GDP. Debt servicing as a percentage of current revenue was 29.3 per cent.

12 In 1979 the SVG Government stopped a Danish consortium taking ownership of Orange Hill Estate (3,200 acres) in the north of St Vincent island after the sale was completed. The estate was at that time the single largest private estate in the country. CRD in Canouan controls some 1,200 acres on a ninety-nine year lease, some 85 per cent of that island.

5

Writing the St Vincent frontier

My perspective on the frontier in this chapter involves an examination of concepts of 'outsider' and 'insider' in relation to St Vincent. While the concerns with 'civilisation' and 'wilderness' persist, they are inflected with the perspectives of the authors whose work I examine. This chapter, then, applies the malleable concept of the frontier to a study of rhetoric, reading the frontier into a variety of written texts concerned with St Vincent. First of these is the journal of the nineteenth-century diarist John Anderson, a stipendiary magistrate recruited to apply the law in the post-slavery apprenticeship period. Then I deal with two novels that offer sketches of St Vincent life: G. C. H. Thomas's fictionalised memoir *Ruler in Hiroona* (1989 [1972]), and Margaret Atwood's thriller *Bodily Harm* (1998 [1981]). While the two novels omit any direct reference to a specific country, they speak strongly to the particularity of the smaller Caribbean islands. Finally, I read two political memoirs by Prime Ministers of St Vincent for what they reveal about the frontier: that of James 'Son' Mitchell, Prime Minister from 1984 to 2001, and the other by his successor, Ralph Gonsalves, who took power in 2001 and is in his fourth term as I write.

This range of literary genres – journal, memoir, novel-as-thriller and novel-as-fictionalised-memoir – gives rise to intriguing inter-textual considerations. Despite disparities in period, narrative perspective, implied readership and authorial position, thematic similarities and common literary devices are strongly suggestive of the way the object represented – the small island society – may be seen to determine key elements of form. For example, John Anderson's journal and Margaret

Atwood's novel are linked by their 'outsider' perspective and the fact they both dramatise difficulties of personal dislocation in a context of ad hoc experimentation in which the (civilised) rules of the society they describe are opaque. However, the two perspectives are clearly dissimilar in fundamental ways. Anderson's colonialist perspective on immediate post-slavery St Vincent society takes for granted his own racial and cultural superiority to its inhabitants, and his own belonging to a regime of domination. His writing is therefore distinguished by distance, the engrained othering of the colonised 'savage' who represents the antithesis of civilised values. For Atwood, a late-twentieth-century postcolonial observer, the distinction between the savage other and the civilised self is less clear-cut. As David Spurr points out: 'As modern civilised human beings, we assert authority over the savage both within us and abroad, but the very energy devoted to such an assertion acknowledges its own incompleteness as authority' (Spurr, 1993: 7). The resulting relative instability of perspective and fracturing of discourse are reflected in Atwood's novel. In place of Anderson's unquestioning power and authority, the outsiderness of Atwood's main character, Rennie, though mediated by privilege, is also burdened by a sense of unease.

In contrast, alongside the 'real' perspectives of the two political memoirs, the novel *Ruler in Hiroona* offers an imaginary insider's perspective on frontier society – that of a small island's Chief Minister, Jerry Mole, who holds political power in the mythical Hiroona for fifteen years. The fact that Thomas's novel parodies a serious memoir makes it a sort of mimic shadow of the two 'real' ones and draws attention to the specificity of the memoir as a form in which the narratorial 'I' guarantees authority and unmediated access to experience and events. When the 'I' is a Prime Minister, that authority is at one level assumed to be incontestable; at another, however, all politics involve the shaping of the truth to suit a particular agenda, and most readers therefore will approach such a narrative with a degree of scepticism. *Ruler in Hiroona* plays with this ambiguity in such a way as to destabilise the 'truth' and expose the depth of political expediency, if not hypocrisy. Thus, the first line of the novel makes clear that this is the authentic testimony of an eastern Caribbean island insider: 'I am committed to tell the stark truth in this autobiography, although this truth is very unflattering to myself' (Thomas, 1989: 1) The setting, too, is deliberately ambiguous, in that it could be any one of the smaller eastern Caribbean islands. Signs, however, point to the specific location being St Vincent, not least the title: 'Hiroona' is the Carib name for St Vincent. Descriptions of the main port and town of 'Kingsland' closely match many features of St Vincent's capital, Kingstown. The trade union leadership path to political power of Jerry Mole offers none-too-subtle a parallel to the career path of St Vincent's first Chief Minister, Ebenezer Joshua, prior to the country's attainment of Associate Statehood with Britain, on the way to full political independence in 1979. The novel suggests that the politician's interest in enhancing Hiroona's 'civilisation' through nation-building is a smoke-screen for a self-seeking career in politics, and its autobiographical form lays out the strategies followed to attain and keep political power. In sum, the fictionalised political memoir is the screen for a behind-the-scenes view of the Vincentian politics of the 1950s and 1960s.

The two real-life memoirs, James Mitchell's *Beyond the Islands* (2006) and Ralph Gonsalves's *The Making of 'The Comrade'* (2010b), offer parallels and contrasts with Thomas's novel. They are texts with implicit frontier retentions told through the political lives of 'pioneering heroes'. All three can be read as extended dialogues with Archie Singham's 1968 analysis of small-island Caribbean politics, *The Hero and the Crowd in a Colonial Polity*, in which he argues that the terminal stage of colonial rule in the region enabled the arrival of a new type of political leader, 'the hero'. He (invariably) was charismatic with Caesarist tendencies combining a host of contradictory traits, including anomie, rage, compulsion and withdrawal. Other characteristics of the pioneering Caribbean national hero conventionally include leadership of national resistance – usually a radical anti-colonial campaign – rising from humble origins and the adoption of self-styled charismatic behaviour. Many of these characteristics are to be found in the pages of the memoirs, both imagined and 'real'.

Outsider perspectives on the St Vincent frontier

Frontier, civilisation and wilderness in John Anderson's journal

When the British Parliament abolished slavery in 1833 this created, in effect, a situation of limbo for some 600,000 people who were no longer slaves but nor were they free. The British colonial authority then introduced an Abolition Act in 1834 that established a period of apprenticeship before full freedom. Apprenticeship was envisaged as a period of training for full freedom but it was a process that was resisted by the actual apprentices. The Act bound ex-slaves to former owners: six years for plantation labourers and four years for domestic and non-field workers. In St Vincent, while planters were compensated £550,777 for loss of labour, the number of slaves freed on the island was 22,266. The average compensation per slave was £26 1s 4d (Levy, 1980: 113). Apprentices were required to labour for forty-five hours per week for their former owners. In return they received the customary payment in kind. Special officials were recruited in Britain to oversee the system.

It was at this point that Scottish-born John Anderson entered the picture. Before he was assigned to St Vincent, he trained in Edinburgh as a lawyer, pursued the life of a gentleman-scholar and achieved a number of publications, prior to keeping the detailed journal of his experiences in St Vincent for the years 1836 to 1838. His journal was never fully completed nor formally published in his lifetime. However, it was edited and annotated by Roderick A. McDonald, professor of history at Rider University, and published with McDonald's annotated comments in 2001.

A helpful point of departure for a discussion of civilisation and wilderness in the context of Anderson's journal, which, because of his relatively short stay in St Vincent, is essentially a form of nineteenth-century metropolitan travel writing, is Mary Louise Pratt's perceptive observation on the nature of the relationship between metropolis and periphery. 'The metropolis', she notes, 'habitually blinds itself to the ways in which the periphery determines the metropolis, beginning, perhaps, with the latter's obsessive need to present and represent its peripheries and its others continually to itself' (Pratt, 1992: 6). These presentations and representations, in the context of colonialism, have often centred on the question 'How are civilisation and wilderness to be negotiated?'. Anderson's journal directly addresses this question.

His diary begins with his departure from Edinburgh in November 1835 and ends abruptly in 1838 following his death from a riding accident. Throughout the diary he determinedly keeps his distance from St Vincent society. In the introductory sections, written during his Atlantic crossing to St Vincent, he first identifies the frontier geographically by recording his responses to nature as he travels south. He invokes the poetics of science while looking at the stars onboard ship. To do this he draws on 'the affecting reflections of Humboldt, – that as we pass from one hemisphere to another, we feel an indescribable sensation in beholding those constellations which we have known in youth, progressively sink, & finally disappear' (McDonald, 2001: 59). But once on land he sees just how wild nature can be: it is, from his perspective, rampant, untamed and untameable because ultimately beyond classification. He observes that:

> The rugged passes present ample range to the botanist, where innumerable species of the vegetable kingdom waste unknown ... Would the admirer of nature gratify his passion to the extreme, let him sweep the leeward shore in a canoe or paragua –. There he will behold her revelling in each alternate form: The wild, – the majestic, – the lovely, – succeed each other in light, in shade so ever varied, – as to make enumeration hopeless.
>
> (McDonald, 2001: 77)

A number of John Anderson's observations on the 'wildness' and chaos of St Vincent and its capital Kingstown have been noted already in an earlier chapter. He is concerned that the 'Great Experiment', as abolition was called, is failing. He suggests that it may take three generations more for the West Indies to 'possess' an 'enlightened and industrious peasantry' (118). Sunday market language is dismissed as a hindrance: 'Long, long indeed will it be', he suggests, 'before this gibberish becomes intelligible to European ears' (75).

The St Vincent frontier is presented in Anderson's journal not only through nature or through social experimentation and flux. The ad hoc nature of society and various forms of personal social dislocation add to the more tangible sense of dislocated frontier living that he conveys. An attempt at formal control of violence by the State in establishing a police force had only recently been established before Anderson's arrival. Such an Act was passed on 23 June 1834, a month and a half after the passage of the Abolition Act 'for Establishing a Police for the Regulation of Apprenticed Labourers'.

St Vincent was sufficiently off the beaten track for Anderson to take considerable pains in his journal to advise prospective visitors what items to bring with them and how to set up home on the island. He lists furniture, linen, types of candle and cloth, and other goods to bring to the island. He offers tips on how to survive the Atlantic crossing and who is untrustworthy in the local building trades. He includes such a list, he claims, because he 'met with such discordant information when on the eve of quitting Europe' and so decided to 'warn such of my friends that may think of a Western trip' (McDonald, 2001: 110).

Just as disquieting as the experience of homemaking is the experience of handling money. Currency variety and speculation simply add to the sense of island chaos in Anderson's view. Currency in circulation as legal tender in St Vincent in the 1830s was a complex mixture, which included the Spanish doubloon (worth $16 or £8 at 1836 prices) and the Portuguese johannesen (or 'joe', valued at half that amount), as well as British pounds sterling, the colonial pound (valued at 4 colonial pounds to £1 14s 8d sterling) and the American dollar (valued at $2 to 1 colonial pound). Colonial silver pieces proportioned into quarters, eighths and sixteenths of a dollar were respectively called 'bits', 'stampees' and 'dogs'. For Anderson, it was a matter of concern which currency was a safer bet and where it should be kept. He observed: 'The gold & silver coins of the Republics of Spanish America, form the current circulation; – for British money is speedily bought up, & remitted to Europe' (McDonald, 2001: 121).

Of course, for Anderson, emotionally the battle was lost from the outset. In the context of 'the charms of the domestic circle', for example, he notes: 'he who treads these Western shores, will soon be reminded he has parted with them, to be a denizen of a land, where discomfort & luxury; where desolation & hospitality, oddly assort'. Ultimately, the wonders of nature on the island and its society compensate 'feebly' for what is left behind in Scotland. He closes a long descriptive list of all that St Vincent has to offer with what, for him, are clearly intended to be damning words: 'we are far from our Fatherland'. The passage reads:

> Feebly does the glowing sky, – and broad matchless bright sea, – sparkling wherever the eye roams, – or the air breathing of jessamine & ponch-pong at nightfall & impregnated with an enervating luxury of existence, – while the moon {swims aloft in a mellowness of splendour unknown in northern latitudes,} looks down in beatick [*sic*] repose – or the hospitable welcome, – or the glass cased lights which illumine the hall, – & the numerous attendants who wait on the festive board, – compensate for what is left behind; – we are far from our Fatherland.'
>
> (McDonald, 2001: 66)

Thus Anderson finds himself in a society in which civilisation is trying to establish its control but is facing the insurmountable odds of the 'wild'.

Frontier, civilisation and wilderness in Margaret Atwood's *Bodily Harm*

A more recent outsider perspective on St Vincent's frontier can be found in the Canadian writer Margaret Atwood's novel *Bodily Harm* (1998 [1981]). It is set partly on the mythical island of St Antoine, and partly in small-town Canada. Atwood is no stranger to St Vincent, particularly its ward island of Bequia in the Grenadines, which she has frequented over many years, forming a friendship with leading politician James 'Son' Mitchell, now retired, and his former wife Pat. Atwood has occasionally published poetry about the island. Her novel traces the thoughts and experiences of her heroine, Rennie Wilford, who describes herself as a 'style journalist'. The reader meets the main character in Canada soon after she has experienced the trauma of a partial mastectomy and the break-up of a long-term relationship. She temporarily flees her metropolitan life in Toronto and obtains a commission to write and take photographs for a travel article about the Caribbean island St Antoine, of which she knows very little. St Antoine's characteristics suggest a thinly disguised late-twentieth-century St Vincent. The novel is set in the weeks after political independence, and involves an aborted secession attempt (a small number of Union Islanders staged just such an attempt to secede from St Vincent in 1979), the killing of a local politician and political manoeuvring around a forthcoming general election. The heroine becomes mixed up unwittingly with drug smuggling and gun running, and, as she is a journalist, is encouraged to report on political electioneering taking place on the island. Rennie also starts a new relationship. She is arrested and thrown into jail with an American acquaintance, Lora, who seems to be more involved with and knowledgeable about the illicit events and the society. The story suggests that Lora dies in jail as a result of a number of rapes and beatings by guards while sharing a cell with Rennie. Atwood's heroine, however, is eventually rescued by Canadian Government diplomatic intervention. She departs the island a changed person, with more self-knowledge and a different perspective than when she arrived. The novel obtained limited attention when it appeared and is viewed as a minor work in Atwood's oeuvre. However, as an outsider's focus on SVG as a frontier society in the late twentieth century, the novel has much to recommend it.

In Atwood's novel, the outsider perspective is suggested by the society's opacity, embodied in the chameleon-like quality exhibited by most of its people. In a discussion about identity in St Antoine, Rennie's lover Paul, who is as much an outsider as he is an insider to the society – an ex-agricultural advisor turned yacht-charterer and smuggler, with connections in local politics – declares: 'Almost nobody here is who they say they are at first. They aren't even who somebody else thinks they are. In this place you get at least three versions of everything, and if you're lucky one of them is true. That's if you're lucky' (Atwood, 1998: 141).

St Antoine's geography and politics are presented as a loose mixture of eastern Caribbean small islands, particularly those of SVG in the late 1970s. The story is told with many intercuttings and flash-backs between life in small-town Griswold, Canada and the small-island Caribbean, capturing and contrasting Rennie's relationships in Canada (with her previous lover, Jake; her doctor, Daniel; and her friend, Jocasta) with those in St Antoine (her lover, Paul; her acquaintance, Lora; and Dr Minnow, a local politician).

In the novel, Atwood avoids conventional lines of demarcation between first world as civilised and third world as wild. The central focus of the novel is Rennie's crisis of identity as a result of the various losses that she has suffered in Canada and her island experiences. In terms of genre, it is clear that such a protagonist is not reliable enough to be the sole narrator, as required in a memoir, fictionalised or otherwise. The third-person narrative perspective of the novel shows the protagonist struggling to re-establish for herself some form of wholeness. Rennie identifies similarities between small-town living in Canada and small-island living, finding each in its own way oppressive. Metropolitan Toronto is as 'wild' or uncivilised as anywhere else. The trigger for Rennie's determination to travel abroad comes after she returns to her apartment to find it broken into, a noose on her bed and detectives already inside the apartment investigating the circumstances of the break-in. The wild, in other words, has invaded her private space and threatens her existence.

Borders and boundaries are as much personal as they are cultural. After her operation, her awareness of her personal frontier between life and death has expanded, though she wants Daniel, her doctor, to clarify the matter for her. 'Either I'm living or I'm dying', she says to him, 'Which is it?' (Atwood, 1998: 52). Though he evades the question, the narrator elaborates on her need for an answer: 'She wants something definite, the real truth, one way or the other. Then she will know what to do next. It's this suspension, hanging in a void, this half-life she can't bear. She can't bear not knowing. She doesn't want to know' (52). Rennie's ambivalence about the nature of this particular boundary arises from the fact that the boundary of her own body has been violated by the cancer that afflicts her. The insecurity of a physical self on which she can no longer rely is metonymic of a spiritual or existential crisis.

Boundaries are also drawn on the basis of misunderstandings, modernity contrasting with quaintness, linguistic misunderstandings and ignorance. These are illustrated in the following exchange between Rennie and a local politician when the small aeroplane in which they are travelling lands at the St Antoine airstrip:

> The plane taxis to a stop and the aisle jams with people. 'It's been nice meeting you', Rennie says as they stand up. He holds out his hand for her to shake ... 'I hope you will have a pleasant stay, my friend. If you need assistance, do not hesitate to call on me. Everyone knows where I can be found. My name is Minnow. Dr Minnow, like the fish. My enemies make jokes about that! A small fish in a small puddle, they say. It is a corruption of the French, Minot was the original, it was one of the many things they left behind them. The family were all pirates.'
>
> 'Really?' Rennie says. 'That's wild.'
>
> 'Wild?' says Dr Minnow.
>
> Fascinating', says Rennie.
>
> Dr Minnow smiles. 'They were common once', he says. 'Some of them were quite respectable; they intermarried with the British and so forth. You have a husband?'
>
> 'Pardon?' says Rennie. The question has caught her by surprise: nobody she knows asks it any more.
>
> 'A man', he says. 'Here we do not bother so much with the formalities.'

Rennie wonders if this is a sexual feeler. She hesitates, 'Not *with* me', she says.

'Perhaps he will join you later?' Dr Minnow says. He looks down at her anxiously, and Rennie sees that this isn't an advance, it's concern. She smiles at him, hoisting her camera bag.

'I'll be fine', she says. Which is not what she believes.

(Atwood, 1998: 22–23)

The novel presents the wilderness element of the frontier in the form of social dislocation. There are boundaries and at times chasms between characters. In this sense civilisation, wilderness and frontier take on a different meaning in Atwood's novel from that in Anderson's journal. Rennie's early exploration of the St Antoine landscape captures her social dislocation when she gets lost in her exploration of the town and encounters a local character:

Rennie walks back on the shadow side. After a few blocks she realizes she's not entirely sure where she is. But she came up to get to the church, so now all she has to do is head down, towards the harbour. Already she's coming to some shops.

Someone touches her on the shoulder, and she stops and turns. It's a man who has once been taller than he is now. He's wearing worn black pants, the fly coming undone, a shirt with no buttons, and one of the wool tea-cosy hats; he has no shoes on, the trouser legs look familiar. He stands in front of her and touches her arm, smiling. His jaw is stubbled with white hairs and most of his teeth are missing.

He makes his right hand into a fist, then points to her, still smiling. Rennie smiles back at him. She doesn't understand what he wants. He repeats the gesture, he's deaf and dumb or perhaps drunk. Rennie feels very suddenly as if she's stepped across a line and found herself on Mars.

(Atwood, 1998: 65)

However, despite this sense of social dislocation, and unlike Anderson (above), Atwood uses Rennie's relentless scepticism to suggest that civilisation and wilderness are not to be found through a simple metropolitan or first world/third world dichotomy. The writing reflects both the privileged outsider's eye, in the detachment with which Rennie observes the beggar on the street, but also incomprehension and unease in her misunderstanding of his gestures and his intention. Does he want to 'bounce' knuckles in friendship or threaten her? The writing is far from reflecting a statement of power in the relationship described. Later in the novel, when Rennie is rescued from jail, her rescuer, an unnamed Canadian diplomat, is described merely as a 'multicultural functionary', though she does recognise the necessity of his role in the assuaging of local egos in order for her to be released from prison.

In this outsider reading of the frontier, Atwood seems to suggest civilisation and its opposite, the wild, if they are anywhere, are located in relationships and how they are conducted. Ultimately, it appears to be the range of experiences that Rennie encounters in St Antoine that give her an ability to focus with which to return to Canada. At the end of the novel, she reflects: 'Zero is waiting somewhere, whoever said there was life everlasting; so why feel grateful? She doesn't have much time left, for anything. But neither does anyone else. She's paying attention, that's all' (Atwood, 1998: 291).

We see then that Atwood's heroine, Rennie, and Anderson, as the recording hand of his journal, despite their different historical contexts, both experience severe social dislocation. The more fundamental difference is that Atwood's Rennie must experience *othering* before she can come to terms with herself; it is therefore an essential ingredient in the remaking of the self after trauma. Anderson's self, in contrast, is buttressed by fussing about what to bring to the island and the use of his journal to keep himself alert, apart and above the rest on the island, as evidenced in this quotation:

> It is astonishing how soon custom reconciles us to habits & feelings the most opposite to our own. Had I – as I was often tempted to do, – given way to this apathetic indifference, I had long ere now have thrown away my pen, and forbore to note down whatever struck me as novel,

or remarkable; but I persevered in spite of heat & lassitude, & ennui, in
hopes I might amuse friends to whom my rough details might prove an
antedote [*sic*] for an idle hour.

(McDonald, 2001: 160)

In both cases, the protagonist/persona at the centre of the narrative is
defined by the fact that they belong elsewhere, a place to which they
will, in due course, return. Meanwhile, a key to the processing of the
otherness of their present condition is the self-reflexive eye that allows
them to project the present scene for the consumption of an audi-
ence at home. In the journal, this is made explicit through the use of
direct address; in the novel, it is implied by the very fact of fictionalisa-
tion – the readership is elsewhere, the consciousness that of a traveller.
However, the purpose of the narrative in each case is quite distinct,
commensurate with the formal dictates of the genre in question, high-
lighting differences of historicity, gender and the development of narrative modes. Such a comparison juxtaposes not only the journal of a
nineteenth-century public servant – a British male, fulfilling an official
mission in a corner of the Empire that, however remote, is nonetheless under his jurisdiction – with a novel about a late-twentieth-century
fictional female protagonist, herself from a former colony, in a state of
existential crisis, but also the formal conventions of these different periods and perspectives. The assumption of the primacy of the integrated
subject – white, male, metropolitan, entitled – gives way to the ambiguity of the modernist fractured self – in this case female, postcolonial – threatened by physical and emotional forces that are as much
internal as external. In both cases, drama is generated by displacement
and liminality, the contest between civilisation and wilderness and the
challenge to subjectivity this imposes.

Insider perspectives on the St Vincent frontier

Like Anderson and Atwood, G. C. H. Thomas examines St Vincent
society at a liminal turning point. While Anderson offers his jaundiced

outsider's perspective on apprenticeship and St Vincent's 1834 post-slavery society, and Atwood sets her novel on the cusp of political independence (for St Vincent in 1979) and around a general election, Thomas chooses the historical moment of the 1950s, the time of constitutional advancement to full adult suffrage for the smaller eastern Caribbean islands.[1] Jerry Mole, Thomas's fictional memoirist, presents his island's political turning point in the following, cynical way:

> Out of this milieu of constitutional advancement, a new type of society and a new type of leader emerged – a leader with a sort of Moses complex, who appeared to regard the local masses as oppressed Israelites, the local Government and the Colonial Office in England being the bad-minded Pharaohs. This 'let-my-people-go' approach to politics provided the political leader with an indispensable reservoir of profitable emotionalism, and it encouraged the masses to put vague, charismatic considerations above intelligence, solid achievement and even integrity, in estimating the worth of some of their political leaders. This was one reason why I was able to achieve such a rapid rise in Hiroona by simply advocating down with this, that and the other, and by preaching the idea of taking over the Government. Demagoguery was the key which opened the door to political leadership.
>
> (Thomas, 1989: 108–109)

One frontier feature that *Ruler in Hiroona* suggests is that increased local political power offers a new form of opportunity for those who can wrestle government power for themselves. Historically, the region and St Vincent had experienced a series of brutal regimes, involving the decimation of the Carib populations, enslavement and indenture within an economy characterised by a racially divided, primitive accumulation form of capitalism with relative extremes of wealth and poverty and subject to the vagaries of the open economy. These regimes prioritised survival and self-advancement while humane feelings were repressed. And so Jerry Mole, seeing his main chance, aims to make the best of his situation having failed at a variety of jobs – clerk, policeman, oil company worker and teacher. He stumbles into politics guided, at first, by

Joe Pittance, his friend and barber. Mole confesses: 'At the outset of my political career, my aim was simply to enter a field in which I thought I could make an easy living and at the same time win local popularity in the role of leader' (Thomas, 1989: 26). Scheming – both petty and exorbitant – quickly becomes routine to ensure self-promotion. He first pockets for himself the compensation that he wins for an injured stevedore. He travels abroad to enhance his *per diem* takings more than to conduct Government business. On a grander scale he uses his position as Chief Minister to enable quid pro quo tax exemptions to business men in return for personal house-building concessions. In the hope of winning a general election he is responsible for destroying by arson a major public-sector business that he fears has become a centre of opposition. Thomas appears to suggest that Mole's frontier political strategies are governed by a desire for personal economic independence and political power that overcomes all scruples.

As befits a frontier story, the narrative comes about because of a wager (that Mole would not dare to write a full and honest autobiography) that he is determined not to lose. Another frontier feature of the novel is the way that men take centre place in the story, presented for the most part as public and political citizens. The scheming Jerry Mole is confronted by his former friend Joe Pittance, who breaks with him and competes for political office. A third opponent is the island's Administrator, Forbes (always kept at a distance, the reader learning only his surname), the British Government's representative. The reader is offered two main sketches of Mole as he grows up. We learn that while he was still young his father absconded and he grew up in a female-headed, single-parent household. He was flogged regularly by his mother as a result of which, it is suggested, he has a mean and vicious streak: at one point he almost drowns a child from his village, for which he is thrashed severely. Mole's adult socialising centres around male political friendships, which are valorised by regular visits to a bar-cum-brothel.

The frontier is traditionally a male preserve, thus in any frontier situation the roles of women, as in this tale, are presented as supportive and subsidiary ones. Mole is elected president of his union, and his wife, Sonia, is elected secretary – as he says, 'You don't want your President to be doing secretary work so I asked my wife if she would help me and of course she agree.' (Thomas, 1989: 40). When their relationship becomes strained – as much from her over-work as from her dislike of the politicking – he is concerned more about the loss of the additional income that she brings in than her health: 'I could not afford to let Sonia give up either of her jobs (Secretary to the Union and Minister of Education and Social Services) although I couldn't help noticing that her holding down the two jobs was doing her health and spirits no good' (Thomas, 1989: 203).

These male and female roles are commonplace in the understanding of Caribbean frontier gender roles. Linden Lewis observes that in social studies, literature and fiction the Caribbean man is invariably presented as 'powerful, exceedingly promiscuous, derelict in parental duties, often absent from the household'. He also notes that the Caribbean man 'has a propensity for female battering, and a demonstrated valorization of alcohol consumption' (Lewis, 2003: 107).

Throughout much of the novel Mole is playing at achieving civilisation – that is, social and economic development. His interest in national development is superficial and it is Sonia who is the conscience of the book. 'You thinking about de big money you making an' de power you have. I thinking about de solid ole friends we losing becarse you feel you too big an' important to take advice from dem' (Thomas, 1989: 291). She points out his devious ways and how the island has hardly advanced under his leadership. ' "De place is exactly the same as when we came into power fourteen years ago", said Sonia. "No improvement. And people don't cultivate arrowroot any more, so de villages look poorer" ' (286). Admittedly, at the outset she accepts the role of Mole's junior partner and the benefits of economic independence that accrue through his political schemes ('three houses in town and one in de country. All rented' (287). However, Sonia tires of the game and threatens to leave him permanently unless he relents. She reprimands him for his devious political manoeuvrings and says

'If politics means doing things like dat, you and politics can go to hell for my part' (292).

The wild or wilderness element of the novel is captured in Jerry Mole's brush with one Margo, who, we are told, had an 'impressive but hush-hush reputation as an obeahwoman' (306). As Mole's plans to defeat his political opponents unravel he begins to fear that he will lose the forth-coming election. In a state of mind that he describes as 'overwrought, confused and troubled' he turns to Margo, who 'sounded competent, convincing, even comforting' (311). Thus he seeks out Margo's divining skills. Obeah in the novel is characterised as the control and manipula-tion of supernatural forces through the use of material objects (dolls dressed like his opponents that he has to prick) and the recitation of spells and ritual bathing that he performs in Margo's house to give him 'canfidence'. The procedures Mole experiences are recounted in consid-erable detail: 'I … was now willing, almost eager, to pay this woman several dollars for what a man in my position should have dismissed as ridiculous hocus pocus, but what I was now convinced was power. Clutching at Margo's straw was proof of my drowning' (312). The prac-tices and charms come to nothing and Mole is routed in the election.

More subtly, Thomas uses the genre of memoir as an apocryphal tale with a civilising mission. His mission is to impart a warning about the nature of politics to Caribbean society. This is bluntly stated and is the central point of the short, four-page concluding section of the novel called 'The Riposte'. No longer interested in even saving face, Mole sees himself as taking on a higher task in writing his autobiography. 'You goin' to expose all yo' dirty linen in a book? What about yo' self-respeck?' Sonia asks him, to which Mole replies: 'Oh, I've thought about that. You have to agree, though, that it takes a hell of a lot of courage and self-sacrifice to tell the truth about yourself to make your country wiser' (336).

The links between the frontier elements in the novelistic memoir of Thomas and the two 'real' memoirs of Mitchell and Gonsalves, though implicit, are, however, easily identifiable. These elements can be seen as much in the generic, charismatic, pioneering hero who centralises power around himself and struggles to implement his version of civilisation through policies aimed at banishing wilderness, disorder and violence. Despite the differences between the career trajectories and ideologies of Mitchell and Gonsalves, a comparison serves to elucidate how far both are driven by the fear of wilderness and the quest for civilisation. They may, indeed, be seen as frontiersmen with the self-appointed mission of pushing back the boundary of wilderness and claiming more space for their own version of civilisation. I will illustrate this by a few specific examples from the career of each man.

Mitchell's travel in Europe in the early 1960s contributed to creating a Cold War warrior with outspoken, anti-communist liberal political views. For example, when he was in office he was happy to be identified as 'one of the sensible ones' by Margaret Thatcher when he was invited to Britain on an official visit. He reminds his readers regularly that he rubs shoulders with the powerful, and throughout his memoir offers lots of 'good advice' based on his religious calling and personal experience. He is also a man of old-fashioned belief in hard work. He writes: 'There is no doubt in my mind that the worst thing slavery did to the Caribbean's people was to leave behind the lingering notion that hard work is to be despised' (Mitchell, 2006: 66).

Alongside his political career, his successful and well-appointed Bequia hotel, the 'Frangipani', played an important role in his politics, as he used it to woo regional and international politicians. The international contacts that he accumulated were to provide access to many loans and grants for economic development. He was responsible, among other infrastructural developments, for land reclamation; land settlement; the building of roads and local airports on Union, Bequia and Canouan; and a cruise ship port for the country. His civilising development programmes did not always run smoothly. An attempt to develop a marina outside Kingstown, at Ottley Hall, proved to be a white elephant that eventually caused the incoming Gonsalves Government to negotiate debt forgiveness. He was particularly proud of his role in the construction of Kingstown's centrepiece, a covered market designed by a foreign architect, to house small traders. This 'civilising' gesture was, however, resisted by many small traders, who preferred to locate their trade on the capital's sidewalks, affording easier access to pedestrians and the avoidance of licence-fee collectors.

Despite his scientific background and public managerial skills as trumpeted in his memoir, in his apparently unceasing battle to push back the wild, Mitchell also acknowledges, occasionally, the challenge of the wilderness – for example its presence in the urban environment. Kingstown's frontier market town quality, where livestock mixed relatively freely with humans, as observed by Frederick Bayley in the nineteenth century, did not disappear quickly. Looking back to 1984, over a century after Bayley's observations, Mitchell complains: 'Pigs had captured the heart of our city, Kingstown. Cattle, too, were flogged through the streets in the commercial district on the way to the abattoir. The pigs and dogs competed for the discarded guts from the fish market. "The poor had to make a dollar" was the justification …' He declares: 'I was not going to preside over a capital city that had remained a pigsty' (Mitchell, 2006: 242).

Mitchell also recounts a painful encounter under his watch with a particular outsider perception of St Vincent: the assumption that its criminal justice system was itself a symptom of the wild frontier. In 1996, a high-profile criminal case involving two yacht-owners from the USA, James and Penelope Fletcher, required Mitchell publicly to defend St Vincent as a 'civilised' legal space. In connection with the violent death of a black, local water-taxi operator, one 'Jolly' Joseph from Bequia, the two Americans were arrested, detained and charged with murder. The case raised the question: can a small, poor country deliver justice to white, wealthy Americans with political connections in the USA? It was apparent from international interest in the case that St Vincent's legal system was as much in the dock as were Mr and Mrs Fletcher. Mitchell appeared on TV in the USA to defend St Vincent's justice system (CNN's *Burden of Proof* and Fox News).[2] American reporters gathered in Kingstown for the trial. President Clinton informally enquired from Mitchell about the conduct of the trial.[3] The accused were eventually released on the judge's ruling that there was no case to answer. In his autobiography Mitchell is critical of the way pressure was brought to bear both in and out of the court to obtain the judge's verdict. He suggests that, in the light of an overheard and recorded religious confession made by Mrs. Fletcher to a priest (though not admitted in evidence), in which she admitted to the murder, due process was observed at the expense of justice. Mitchell presents the experience of defending St Vincent's system of due legal process as one of 'fac[ing] up to America in order to preserve our integrity and way of life' (Mitchell, 2006: 386).[4] In a telling aside that more directly captures the frontier element that the case exposed, Mitchell concludes from the experience: 'Small states are not always recognized as nations. Seeking to extend the destiny of a small state was always an encounter with reality' (386).

For his part, in his memoir Gonsalves offers an uninhibited, frontier-style account, first of his early years; then of his time in regional radical left-leaning politics, first as a student and later as political party activist; and then of his period as Prime Minister for two terms of office. His text goes on to offer a bullet-point list of achievements from his time in office and a manifesto for his third term – which he won (he has since entered a fourth term in office). As discussed earlier, Gonsalves is a public champion of the notion of 'Caribbean civilisation'. More specifically, he presents himself as ideologically in marked contrast to Mitchell though with a similar civilising zeal, which, he argues, is in the interest of 'our people's humanization' and inflected by 'a genuine love for the poor, their upliftment and their quest for a more profoundly democratic politics' (Gonsalves, 2010b: 102). His popular nickname, 'the Comrade',[5] signals his ideological distance from Mitchell.[6] While Mitchell befriended conventional western backers to pursue St Vincent's development, Gonsalves chose to forge links with Venezuela, Bolivia and Cuba as well as countries in the Middle and Far East. He advocates this strategy as a 'progressive and enlightened policy not interested in what the State Department thinks, but concerned to realize the best interests of his people'. These initiatives, he humbly suggests, reflect his 'uninhibited and magnetic personality' (Gonsalves, 2010b: xiii).

Since Gonsalves combines the authority of an intellectual eastern Caribbean leader with a determination to follow his own diplomatic, aid and foreign policy paths, it is hardly surprising that American State Department analysts have taken an interest in his activities. In one report, he is described as 'easily the most intelligent and charismatic' of eastern Caribbean leaders and a 'mercurial' and 'pragmatic ideologue', as well as a 'master of contradiction' with a strong populist spirit and socialist ideology. Against this mixed bag of compliments are weighed more critically his management style[7] and his 'peccadilloes'.[8]

Born in 1946, Gonsalves is proud to trace his roots to a peasant background in the St Vincent countryside. His memoir charts his heroic path from hard times to scholarship-winning academic and left-leaning political activist, before entering St Vincent party politics. In his civilising role as Prime Minister he boasts of poverty eradication and mass education drives under his leadership.[9] Opponents are described as 'divisive 'and 'unpatriotic' while those he admires are invariably 'titans'. He has pinned considerable hope and resources to his flagship project, the building of an international airport.[10] In a more personal civilising gesture, Gonsalves has chosen to publicise his Catholicism, has held audiences with three Popes – John Paul II, Benedict and Francis – and has published *Diary of a Prime Minister* (2010a), which records his 'ten days among Benedictine monks' at the Mount St Benedict retreat in Trinidad.

How is the frontier to be interpreted through the lives of these two self-dramatising political leaders? Unlike Thomas's character Jerry Mole, neither Mitchell nor Gonsalves needed politics to establish personal economic independence. Both 'real' politicians were professionals with independent incomes, Gonsalves a practising criminal lawyer and Mitchell an agricultural scientist and successful hotelier in Bequia. The masculinity of their frontier style is apparent in that in each instance women play supportive and subsidiary roles in their lives. Indeed, both Mitchell and Gonsalves emphasise the sacrifice their respective families have made for their respective causes. Despite their ideological and personality differences, unlike Jerry Mole, Mitchell and Gonsalves take seriously their civilising roles in developing the society.

Each memoir is a tale of a self-styled, distinctive grand pioneer exercising autonomy and power. Each practises his 'David' strategies to pursue the interests of their small island state against the 'Goliaths' of the modern world. Mitchell, through his hotel, woos wealthy western governments and developers; Gonsalves mixes socialist rhetoric with pragmatic economic interest and establishment religion. Both keep under their control decision-making authority and access to information – the office of Prime Minister includes leadership of the ministries of finance, national security, economic planning and legal affairs. The result, one critic observes, makes small governing institutions even smaller. Both regimens have from time to time relied on litigation to intimidate local media outlets. Finally, a noticeable difference between the writing of Thomas in his novel and that of the 'real' autobiographies is the ironic inflection invested in Thomas's writing, which contrasts with the seriousness and self-importance of the two 'real' memoirs.

Notes

1 St Vincent obtained universal adult suffrage on 5 May 1951.
2 For a summary of the critically damning episode of the US TV programme *Nightline* about SVG, as well as an even-handed overview of the issues, see Barich (1997).
3 For Mitchell's presentation of the discussion with Clinton see Mitchell (2006), 384; and for his perspective on the case see 382–386.
4 Gonsalves, then a defence lawyer for Mr Fletcher, was critical of Mitchell's 'awful' media performances. For his perspective on the case and the issues raised see Gonsalves (2010), 117–20.
5 Gonsalves associates his nickname with 'solidarity and struggle on behalf of the poor and working people'. In contrast, Thomas reflects on the history of the term from when it was popularised in the political circles of the 1950s, describing it as 'a new nice-sounding word that had the same effect on certain adults that the gift of cheap candy has on the children of peasants' (Thomas, 1989: 28).
6 Unsurprisingly, there was little love lost between these two political opponents. Mitchell describes Gonsalves (before the latter was Prime Minister) as 'a prominent local criminal lawyer well established in the defense of drug dealers in the region' (Mitchell, 2006: 383). In turn, Gonsalves refers to Mitchell as 'a dangerous reactionary spirit in the body politic' (Gonsalves, 2010b: 103).

7 One comment notes that in small Caribbean countries 'decision-making and access to information are often concentrated in a small clique close to the prime minister. In St Vincent, PM Gonsalves has taken this tendency to an extreme.' https://wikileaks.org/plusd/cables/06BRIDGETOWN554_a.html (accessed 2 August 2016).

8 The same profile claimed that it is 'undisputed that Gonsalves abused his position as National Security Minister and his personal relationship with the Public Prosecutor to circumvent the rule of law and ensure that rape charges were never filed against him'. In all the cases brought Gonsalves protested his innocence. In his autobiography he summarised the legal challenges he faced and the legal outcomes, concluding 'I stood firm on my innocence, did the work for which I was elected, and allowed the legal process to exhaust it' (Gonsalves, 2010b: 360).

9 'Perhaps', Gonsalves writes, 'no achievement of the Comrade ranks higher in terms of its human impact, and the short term and long term implications for the enrichment of the country' (Gonsalves, 2010b: xii).

10 Gonsalves identifies St Vincent's new international airport as essential for development. Mitchell argues that there are already four international airports in a radius of 200 miles of St Vincent.

6

Shifting rural and urban frontiers
in St Vincent

Territorially small though St Vincent may be, the frontier between ('wild') hinterland country and ('civilised') urbanity is reinforced by the island's complex and difficult topography. The natural wild persists in twenty-first century St Vincent in its hills and central mountainous terrain. Numerous divisions, spurs and folds slice through either side of the island's central spine of mountains separating leeward and windward coasts. A giant could hop along this spine from one central volcanic peak to the next and so work his way along the length of the island from south to north. His last step would end at La Soufriere, the island's active northern volcano, which rises to 1,234 m (4,048 ft). The extinct volcanic peaks to the south of La Soufriere are named Richmond at 993 m (3,528 ft); Petit Bon Homme, 756 m (2,481 ft); and Mt St Andrew, 735.5 m (2,413 ft). The southern coastline, not without its hills, is however flatter and more gently sloping. The population of St Vincent has been increasingly concentrated in the south of the island, particularly Kingstown and its environs. The concentration suggests that the same hopping giant has stood the island on its southern tip and shaken it vigorously so that most of the island's population has gathered around the southern coastal rim. The island's most southerly census district of Calliaqua contains the single largest population by far of the whole island. In 2007 the total was 20,844 (22.6 per cent of St Vincent's population): almost twice the next largest census district, the suburbs of Kingstown, where for 2007 the total was 11,800.[1]

On the flanks of the hillsides, spurs – steep, sharply crested and serrated, with deeply folded ravines locally known as 'gutters' – fan out
towards coastal bays or drop precipitously to the sea. These ravines
were gouged by pyroclastic lava flows from intermittent volcanic eruptions through the centuries. The eruptions poured out *nuée ardente* –
the 'glowing clouds' that asphyxiate humans and animals and burn the
bush cover – while hot lava gouged deep furrows down the flanks of the
volcano to either coastline. As a result, to reach the capital in the south
from the (leeward) western shores, people travelled by large, many-
oared canoes well into the twentieth century. This could be a hazardous
journey. Depending on sea swells and boat loads the boats occasionally capsized, drowning produce and passengers alike. The intermittent volcanic activity also created black sand beaches around much of
the island's coastline. Completing a road network circling the entire
island remains a challenge, with the road at present petering out near
Richmond in the north-east – another reminder of continuing hinterland. The windward (east) side of the island is flatter and more gently
sloping, though as it faces the Atlantic it is exposed to the north-east
trade winds and heavy swells.

The urban landscape, meanwhile, constitutes the island's para-
doxical encounter with modernity. At the western end of the town,
before the climb towards the leeward coast, are the island's historical Botanical Gardens, among the oldest in the western hemisphere.
Their 21 acres (8.5 ha) remain a colonial legacy of scientific trans-
plantation of plant species from locations as far away as Tahiti,
including Captain Bligh's famous breadfruit. Now under-funded and
neglected, the gardens remain, nonetheless, an enduring urban statement that wild nature can be organised, tamed and conquered. At
the eastern end of Kingstown lies the deep-water harbour (reclaimed
from the sea) with its spotless entrance and tourist-beckoning bou-
tiques, though even in the tourist season only the occasional liner
calls. The street leading to and from the port is lined by a mixture of dilapidated shops, an ageing supermarket, a recently built

glass-and-concrete modern public building and derelict homes. Lorries, vans and wooden hand-made push-carts compete for road space. In one side-street in mid-town you can find a wine shop with a few bottles of *Chateau Haut-Brion Penac* red from the year 2000 on sale for EC$4,792.31 per bottle. Across the street stands the Salvation Army Building with day nursery, clothes bank and infant feeding programme.

Artist and activist Vonni Roudette claims that nature has been defeated in the capital. She writes:

> Moving into the city itself and all signs of nature have gone; the last piece
> of greenery in the town centre was destroyed by the construction of the
> Central Market several years ago. Every mature tree in town has been
> ruthlessly cut down. From here in the city, the mountain background
> seems like another world, nature is excluded totally from town culture.
>
> (Roudette, 2009: 27)

This, however, overlooks the social dimension of the relationship between countryside and town. Instead of retreating from the town, at least two ('wild') social influences from the hinterland have taken up residence in the island's centre of urbanity and 'civilisation'.

My first example of this process is the increasing acceptability of the 'Wilderness People', as they were known in the nineteenth century, as an urban presence. The Spiritual or Shaker Baptists, as they became known, were officially banned altogether for some sixty years for religious practices that alarmed mainstream colonial society (though the ban was enforced for less than half of that time). My second example is the changing attitudes towards marijuana use and supply in early-twenty-first-century St Vincent. The two are linked by establishment attempts at banning, followed by a coming-to-terms with these social aspects of the Vincentian hinterland. While the incorporation of Shaker Baptists into mainstream society has long been complete, the acceptability of marijuana growing and use remains a work in progress.

Spiritual Baptists and the shifting frontier of religious acceptability

[A]fter hymns and prayers come the part which is called Rejoicing. This consists of songs set to dance music, which cause them to shake and jump about in the most awful manner possible, in their frenzied state they make use of words which they call the 'unknown tongue', said to be known and understood by them alone.[2]

This description of Shaker ritual captures some of the fear and anxiety that the religious sect excited in St Vincent, resulting in the Shaker Prohibition Ordinance in 1912. The ban was actively prosecuted till around 1935, after which regulation lapsed until it was officially revoked in 1965. Vincentian historian Adrian Fraser suggests that Spiritual Baptists may have been active before emancipation among the slave population of the island (Fraser, 2011: 18). British historian Sheena Boa claims more specifically that around 1846 a new religious group was formed near the Calder estate in the central windward district calling itself the Wilderness People, for a time also known as 'Penitents' and the 'New Light' movement. The name 'Shakers' was given to them by their early critics and has stuck, although they are now officially 'Spiritual Baptists'. Patricia Stephens, a practising Spiritual Baptist, emphasises the sect members' sense of a link to the spiritual world. Rites include dancing to placate dead ancestors as well as food offerings. The 'Shaker' or shaking aspect that concerned outsiders have focused on is represented by Stephens as the use of the body like a musical instrument, as opposed to drums, which were forbidden. Both historians accept that many who joined the Shakers were probably at one time members of St Vincent's (Wesleyan) Methodist congregations. Methodist ministers were the most active missionaries ministering to the enslaved population on plantations, and they exercised strict control over their flock. They opposed dancing and drumming and operated a strictly conservative morality with regard to sexual relations (Boa, 1998).

The Wilderness People found the services of the Methodists staid and unacceptable as a form of worship.[3] Methodist missionary ministers, meanwhile, were disgusted by the practices of these dissenters, whose behaviour they considered to be out of control. Among the uncontrollable elements cited were indulgence in trance and 'speaking in tongues', induced by long periods of abstinence and of dancing. In addition, by holding services in the open air Shakers combined these unacceptable rituals with the physicality of nature and the wild, thus putting themselves beyond the easy reach of those in authority. One result of this combination, it was vaguely suggested, was sexual orgies. For example, the Methodist Revd Hurd observed that Shakers were 'in the habit of going into the woods to hold prayer meetings, which were generally continued all night and provided the fruitful source of great irregularities and crime' (Boa, 1998: 265). The new sect soon became a direct threat because it poached members from Methodist congregations and, by the early 1900s, had established thirty-eight separate meeting houses. By 1905, Fraser suggests, some 90 per cent of Shaker congregations were composed of renegade Methodists. Another unsettling challenge was that Shakers implemented gender equality in leadership roles. Both men and women could preach at meetings and interpret 'speaking in tongues', and many women held ceremonial roles, including operating as 'Shepherdesses' of prayer houses. These independent innovations contrasted with an exclusively masculine Methodist missionary body answerable to General Secretaries in England, and the relegation of women to minimal roles concerned with the upkeep of churches. Another feature of the sect that did not endear it to the establishment was that it long remained a rural, black, peasant-led organisation[4] with links to African cultural and behavioural retentions.[5] It was perceived as a rural threat because it was independent of European influence and beyond establishment control. The identification of Shaker practice with African cultural retentions added to the generalised moral panic of the respectable authorities. Thus the 1905 report of the Acting Chief of Police on the

Shakers claimed that they exhibited 'one of the few distinct hereditary traits of African barbarism which still remains to the Black race of St Vincent' (quoted in Fraser, 2011: 19).

After a number of police and Church-based reports on their activities, the Shakers were banned under the colony's Shakerism Prohibition Ordinance in 1912. In introducing the legislation, the island's Administrator described the threat that practitioners posed as 'a blot on our civilisation and a stain on the history of the Colony'. The Ordinance made it an offence 'to hold or take part in or attend any Shaker meeting to be held in any part of the colony, indoors or in the open air at any time of day or night'.[6] Prosecutions may be assumed to have taken place regularly from the early years of the ban, though only the numbers prosecuted from 1920 until 1934 are available. In 1934 some ninety-four sect members, the largest number in any one year, were convicted.

To avoid prosecutions most of the Shaker prayer houses were located in the countryside, and for a while participants avoided Kingstown. However, by 1935, as official interest in prosecuting sect members declined, meetings began to be held in the capital. This easing of prosecution coincided with an active campaign led by George McIntosh to remove the official ban. McIntosh owned and operated a pharmacy in one of the poorer areas of the capital. He was widely recognised as a spokesman for the poor and was elected as leader of the Workingmen's Association in the colony's Legislative Council. He championed the right of Shakers to practice religious observance in their own way and put forward two formal proposals to the island's Council for the repeal of the Ordinance. Both efforts were vetoed by the authority of the (appointed) Executive Council but it may well be that the political pressure he applied was enough to ease the formal persecution of the Shakers. In 1950, the burial ceremony of one of their Shepherdesses was preceded by a march through Kingstown. The occasion was celebrated by the poet Shake Keane, in his poem 'Mistress Mucket's Funeral', later called 'Shaker Funeral':

Shaker Funeral

Sorrow sin-
bound, pelting din
big chorusclash
o' the mourners;
[…]
>   Sweet Mother gone
>   to the by and by,
>   follow her to the brink o' Zion …

Wave wave
as they roared to grave
a drench song –
soulthunder –
was *aymens* through
the wind, shrieks flew,
and the eyes were strong;
for 'twas madness gave
them dirge, that grew
made thunder.

Drums, flags,
pious rags o'
robes stanching
sweat;
mitre o' tattered
straw, bamboo crozier
wagged by wind's clenching –
deathwind that bragged
sorrow, smattered
o' sweat.
>   Saints in blue
>   bathrobes flew
>   about the ranks o' the sinners,
and froth-lipped virgins
with powdered skins
and frocks that stank
with the slime and the stew
from the purged away sins
o' the sinners;

And heads were white
in starch cloth … Bright
was the blood from the eyes
o' the candles;

and the 'horn of the Ram
of the great I Am'
spoke hoarse in cries ...
and crowned with the light
o' the Judah Lamb
were the candles.

     Lord delivered Daniel
     from shame's mouth,
     (o strong, o strong roll Jordan),
     Lord deliver our Mother
     gone to the Glory Home,
     gone to the Glory Home, gone to Zion.

All God's brothers
were loud, and the ten
holy lampers were
reeking in smoke;
and the 'valley of sod-and-shadow',
Staff-Rod,
was blenched as the cankering
sweat o' men
and the reeking o' God
in the smoke.

     His willing be,
     Mother gone,
     Jordan deep,
     but her soul is strong.
     Follow her to the brink o' Zion.

And now the grave
was washed in a wave
o' wails and a
city o' stars

that dribbled and burned
in the tears that turned
hot sins, on the smoke-white pillars ...
But their sorrow was yells,
And their faith was brave
as the blood-blemished lambs
piled big on the grave
their city o' wax and stars.

     Sweet Mother gone,
     King o' Mansions-over-Jordan.

O strong …
Leave her safe on the brink o' Zion.
(Brown and McWatt,
2005: 97–99)

In 1951 St Vincent achieved full adult suffrage and by 1967 achieved
Associated Statehood with Great Britain. This intermediate status,
between colony and full political independence, gave the State the right
of full control over its internal affairs. The Ordinance banning Shaker
practices was finally repealed in 1965, tabled by the island's first Chief
Minister, Ebenezer Joshua, with no dissenters. A further indication
of the acceptance of the sect lies in its inclusion as one of twelve religious denominations regularly recorded in the national census counts
since 1960. Its membership increased between 1960 and 1991, and then
showed little change during the following census years. With a substantial decline in Methodist Church membership, by 2012 Shaker and
Methodist numbers were at a similar level.[7]

The shifting frontier of marijuana tolerance

As a result of the natural wildness imposed by geography on the St
Vincent countryside, attempts to expunge the wild through the management of social and economic countryside practices constituted a night-
mare for both colonial and postcolonial governments. The slow death of
the St Vincent sugar industry during the nineteenth century created conditions so desperate for the mass of the rural workforce that by the end
of the century, State acquisition of land for small farmers was officially
recommended. This process was begun in 1899. However, the beginnings
of land settlement brought to light a conundrum. As David Eltis points
out, if civilisation was to be located anywhere in the countryside it was
assumed to lie in large-scale agriculture and not small peasant-held plots.
In 1882, for example, an estimated two-thirds of the island – twenty-two
estates – were owned by a single owner, one D. K. Porter, while a further
sixteen estates were owned by three other planters.

At the end of the nineteenth century the overriding colonial anxiety alongside the apparent need for the development of small farms was the fear of a regression to what the authorities called 'African livelihood patterns'. This notion was open to a variety of negative interpretations, including low moral standards in unsupervised areas of settlement.[8] The historian Bonham Richardson noted that in 1890, when St Vincent's Governor, Sir Walter Hely-Hutchinson, was assessing locations in the north-west of the island with a view to providing grants for small settlements near to Richmond Valley, he was anxious to ensure that such settlements would remain under Government supervision. The reason for this anxiety, as Richardson notes, was that 'he had observed near-naked women, a sure sign of immorality and decadence' (Richardson, 1997: 220).[9]

As St Vincent's large private landowners lost interest in their ailing plantations, the Government increasingly bought them, becoming, by the 1960s, the island's largest landowner. Over the years a variety of smallholder land settlement schemes have been implemented with mixed results. Crown lands on forested slopes in the centre of the island – that is, above 107 m (350 ft) – have long been officially protected for water conservation and to stop soil erosion. At the same time, the trees on the upper reaches of these hillsides have long been felled and burnt for charcoal, or the land squatted for banana growing. Deforestation then has been a problem for many years, recently exacerbated by clandestine marijuana growing and use.[10]

In the latter part of the twentieth century a legitimate, if protected, trade in banana growing, which was equally popular with small as well as large farmers, became increasingly uneconomic as British and European Union subsidies to the eastern Caribbean were dismantled as a result of World Trade Organization regulations. From around 9,000 registered banana farmers in St Vincent in the early 1990s, who employed 10,000 people on a weekly basis, there were by 1998 no more than 4,500 registered. By the 1990s the alternative cash-crop economy of marijuana growing began to thrive in the protected 'wildness' or upper reaches of the island's hinterland. By 1999 St Vincent was the major trafficker in the southern part of the region. Estimates by the UNDP suggest that for this year the island supplied 7,180 kg. The next highest supplier was Barbados with 333 kg (Klein, 2004: 225). One estimate suggests that at the turn of the century close to one-fifth of the island's GDP was raised through illegal marijuana sales and exports (Fineman, 2000). By 2002 there were an estimated 1,500 marijuana farmers culti-vating in excess of 1,200 ha (*c*. 3,000 acres (1,214 ha)) in the northern St Vincent hills (John, 2006: 13). The growers supplied a regional and local market. The social anthropologist Axel Klein has spent time with some of these farmers in the St Vincent hills observing their patterns of cultivation and crop sales. He describes them as rugged individu-als for whom 'Insecurity is the hallmark of ganja cultivation at every step of the cycle' (Klein, 2004: 230). They are confronted with the pros-pect of thieves, eradication from coordinated military and police raids, ambush from rivals, and being cheated by buyers. They are in many ways, then, identifiable as modern frontiersmen in all but name.

These developments produced the knock-on effects of soil erosion, rapid run-off of water and lack of soil absorption. Government attempts to eradicate what has become a small-scale industry by arrests of users and growers as well as crop eradication (burning) were failing and causing a loss of popular political support. By 2002 more incorporative strategies, less concerned with eradication and more concerned with forest protection, were devised. Both language and strategies began to change. An 'integrated forest management and rural livelihoods project' was developed for farmers who were no longer referred to as 'squatters' or 'illegal growers' but 'forest users'. Incentives for replanting of trees for forest cover were initiated. It is a moot point how committed national authorities, especially politicians, were to forest protection and ganja eradication.[11] With increasing availability of ganja on the capital's doorstep, supplied through the island's mini-van network,[12] the use of the herb in Kingstown has become not unusual. This process operates to the extent that suppliers and users in various parts of the capital can exploit a 'blind eye' space between official illegality and a degree of pub-lic use.

Official negotiation between 'civilised' Government authority and illegal growers and other squatters – the latter increasingly recognised in the bland terms such as 'forest users' – increasingly emphasise strategies to enhance forest protection. Elsewhere in the region, Jamaica has started the process of decriminalising possession of small amounts of ganja. Ralph Gonsalves, the SVG Prime Minister, initiated discussion at the 2014 CARICOM Heads of Government meeting of its legalisation for medical use. An investigative report for the agency was commissioned.

Junior Spirit Cottle: St Vincent's marijuana pioneer

I not shy to open my mouth to talk.
Junior Cottle

A tall wisp of a man in his mid-sixties dressed in jeans and sandals, with Rasta locks and a straggly beard, the one-time chairman of St Vincent Marijuana Growers' Association now describes himself as 'retired'. Mostly self-educated, he became politically active in the 1970s during the St Vincent Black Power movement. In 1973 he was accused with two others (Lorraine 'Blackie' Laidlaw and Marcus 'Raycan' James) of shooting and killing Cecil Rawle, the acting Attorney General of SVG. Rawle was shot in his home and died three days later in hospital. Before being captured, Cottle was shot in the neck while being pursued by the police. The bullet, he tells me, remains lodged in him, to no apparent distress. In October 1973 Cottle was convicted for Rawle's murder and sentenced to be hanged. After a number of appeals his case reached the British Privy Council in 1976. The conviction for murder was revoked on account of irregularities in the 1973 trial. He was then rearrested for another offence: firing a gun at a police corporal, for which he served eleven years. He used this period in jail (1973 to 1984) to educate himself, mainly by reading Karl Marx. After the Government and international agencies' ganja crop elimination drive in 1998, called 'Weedeater', Cottle led a march of ganja growers in Kingstown to protest Government action. As well as being a political activist and campaigner for legalising marijuana growing and use, he has at various times in his life been a farmer, Government Agricultural Department employee, and liaison officer between marijuana growers and forest rangers. He thus became eventually a literal frontier, liminal character, who has swung between the wild and officialdom.

Cottle now owns a 'flowers shop' at the corner of Western Bridge and Bay Street on the edge of Bottom Town. His shop sells plants, while doubling, more actively on my visit, as a down-town bar. A wooden seat curves around the inside of the small bar-room with a few stools at the bar itself: Rasta colours painted inside, green paint on the outside wall. The west side of the bar is surrounded by plants on the outer perimeter. The bar is well stocked with a range of alcohol. On the afternoon that we meet there, around ten young people sit around the room. Bottled Guinness and (the local) Hairoon beer are the most popular drinks. The atmosphere is thick with ganja smoke and loud, heavy reggae. Everyone has to shout to be heard. Home-made spliffs are openly smoked. Cottle sits close to me cradling one, a polystyrene cup of soup and two beers between us (his soup, he says, to counter a skin condition). He speaks in a thick Vincentian working-class accent with a raspy, smoke-filled voice that at times slurs his words.

Now, in another manifestation, he has become an articulate, working-class intellectual. He has written a number of articles arguing for acceptance of ganja use and legalisation of the growing of the plant. He has jointly authored official investigations that examine causes of deforestation. He claims to have moved on from the local liaison job between growers and (Government-employed) forest rangers. Professing retirement, he liaises as an official civil society representative for a number of international agencies. In 2009 he attended the First Global Forum on Cannabis, Opium and Poppy Cultivation in Barcelona. This was part of the UN Special Session on Drugs. He shows me the document stating his election to the Second Global Forum Steering Committee and his invitation to attend the Informal Drug Policy Dialogue, 23–25

April 2015. This group will in turn report to the April 2016 UN Special Session on Drugs.

He identified three areas where he is active: encouraging the recognition of the general benefits of marijuana for medical purposes, decriminalisation of its use and possession, and recognition that the herb provides a legitimate alternative livelihood.

He argued that the acceptance of the legitimate growing of the herb will help to preserve the forest through a replanting programme. He is convinced that in the country's forthcoming general election in 2016, 'No politician will speak out openly against it [marijuana use] in St Vincent.' Junior Spirit Cottle is a forceful intermediary between hinterland growers and urban local (and international) officialdom. His activities exemplify the role of a pioneer negotiating the shift between 'wild' hinterland production and urban 'civilised' acceptance of what remains an illegal, but increasingly uncontrollable, form of economic and social development in the St Vincent hinterland and capital.[13]

Struggles to maintain 'civilisation' and contain Kingstown's urban 'wilderness'

As a visitor once noticed, Kingstown has few buildings taller than a coconut tree. It is a noisy, bright market town with too many cars and countless higglers (street vendors) each planted on their patch of pavement tending their heaps of fruit or vegetables. The Little Tokyo bus stand is one of two in the capital full of vans idling and spewing petrol fumes as they wait for passengers, or revving already hot engines for the next trip to the countryside.

Urban living quickly took over from the plantation estates as the nearest thing to civilisation afforded by the island. But, if keeping order is a test of civilisation, then for the town wilderness encroachment is a ceaseless challenge. On a recent visit to Kingstown I spoke with Maurice Baisden, a local archaeologist. His family has lived in the capital for generations. We spoke about how the town had changed over the

years, especially the suburbs growing out of the legitimising of squatting by the Government's offer of land rights in the New Montrose or
'Monkey Hill' area, and more recent suburbanisation in the environs
above and to the east of the town, through the sale of lots to private buyers in the Cane Garden area. We sat on the steps of the town's Central
Library one afternoon while he told me about his grandfather, once a
town warden in the capital. At the turn of the twentieth century, town
wardens were employed by the local-government Town Board to keep
order in Kingstown. They were responsible for ejecting people who
were not from the town before its gates were closed in the evening –
the town was small enough for them to know who 'belonged' and who
didn't. During the day a part of the warden's job was to regulate hig-
glering, limiting where it could take place and enforcing the collection
of dues and licences from vendors. If vendors strayed from the market
area in the centre of town, the warden was authorised to confiscate their
wooden stalls and keep their produce long enough for the goods to rot
and thus become useless for sale. This would happen frequently till the
unregulated vending stopped.

Today, an Italian-designed, concrete-covered market has replaced
the last patch of green in the town centre. Hot and under-used, the
market is an unpopular location for fruit- and vegetable-sellers.
Meanwhile, street vending continues for the most part unchecked
across town. There are also cheap, bootlegged CDs and DVDs on sale,
and card sharps plying their trades. Street vendors may also sell a store
owner's stock outside the owner's premises. The Government and Town
Board prefer to collect taxes and licence fees from itinerant vendors
(street vending is charged a cheaper rate than in the covered market)
rather than move them on. On the more popular and central public
pedestrian pavements pitches on both sides of the pavement com-
pel pedestrians to walk in its centre. There are occasional attempts to
move vendors – for example near to election time – but unless licence
fees are being collected the vendors stay put. For many years Heritage
Square, in the town centre, had only one regular vendor of alcohol on
the street. The area is a popular location at carnival and other festive

times, and so temporary stalls would also be set up along this stretch, ranged along the town centre's riverbank beside the Central Library. These temporary vendors have now become numerous and permanent. On Friday evenings, public 'blocko' fetes catering to all comers take over the central square, the scent of illegal marijuana hovering over the square while police patrol its outer limits. In this way, boundaries and borders become confused, as, for a time each week, ganja moves to the centre, while law and order patrol the periphery.

Figures on the front line 1: the 'queen of Bottom Town'

Shirley Lynch is over seventy years old. She has lived for over forty years in an area of Kingstown known colloquially as 'Bottom Town'. There is no official area so described. It is a beach side area of west Kingstown that is notorious as one of the rougher corners of the capital. To an outsider, the area appears to be a somewhat down-at-heel urban fishing village on the town's western outskirts before one takes the climb to the more salubrious Edinboro district along the coast or moves inland to Montrose and the leeward stretch of the island. In the 1970s, the Government reclaimed some 18 acres (7.3 ha) of land from the Kingstown harbour and along the bay front, incorporating this area of Kingstown. Before the reclamation the front of Shirley's house looked onto the black-sand beach and out to sea. When the weather was rough the sea came up to her door and occasionally flooded the ground floor. Some houses in the neighbourhood have turned their frontages into small grocery and rum shops. On the reclaimed land there are also a bar, and communal shower and toilet facilities. Bottom Town and its environs are where newcomers from the countryside often begin their urban life. Though over the years the area has gained a reputation as a violent and dangerous part of Kingstown, residents are protective of it. As Shirley Lynch says of outsiders: 'We don't look for trouble, but if someone comes looking for trouble they will find it.'

I have known Shirley for some fifty years. It was in the role of employer that my father took on a young Shirley Lynch as his administrative assistant. Growing up in a household where adults were authoritarian and could be volatile, I found her a warm and reassuring presence. She, in turn, treated me with respect and kindness, and out of that grew the friendship that has endured to this day. In the late 1960s, while I was a schoolboy in Kingstown, for about ten years she worked as a young administrative assistant in my parents' businesses – the insurance agency my father ran and the sale of Avon cosmetics coordinated by my mother. Both required someone who could be trusted, and she fitted the bill. Prior to that job she had been a primary school teacher in a small private school run by her aunt, located on the same spot that she now occupies with her family. After leaving my family's employment, she got a job in the smocking industry. This was an early attempt to create an economic zone of household rural employment by using seamstresses around the island to finish partly completed garments before re-exporting them to the USA. As a fieldwork manager she controlled the outsourcing of garments to be sewn in individual homes across the island, collecting the completed work which was then re-exported. Although I left the island when I was thirteen, such was the bond between us that I would visit her at home when I returned. Strained by lack of contact, sometimes lasting for years, that bond was never finally broken. As I have renewed my links with more frequent visits to St Vincent in the past twelve years, the contact has been re-established. A recent visit was along the following lines:

> Side veranda, concrete-wall house located in Bottom Town, the notoriously rough end of Kingstown, capital of SVG. Supplicant in khaki shirt, with grey balding head, has his back to me. He stands just below the level of the veranda, his eyes level with the desk-top that stands on the veranda floor. He is speaking with an elderly lady known to all around as Mother Lynch. She is a sprightly, seventy-something black woman with short, greying plaits. She wears a nightgown, slippers and spectacles,

through which she stares at him without expression. Mother Lynch sits upright at her battered school-desk, on which rest two sturdy elbows, her Bible and a well-thumbed school exercise book. She holds the stub of a pencil in one hand. She is stoic, silent and expressionless. Khaki-shirt has come for an 'ease', a loan. Business concluded, he turns to go. I step over one of the knee-high metal wicket gates as Khaki-shirt exits over the other gate nearest to him. I call her name. She looks up, beams, stands and gives me a hug. We pick up where we left off and gossip about family. Who's doing what? Where are they? No dialect or nation language here – strictly Standard English, she with her certainties and her school mistress adages:

'Stay and shelter from the rain, it will soon stop. Two wrongs don't make a right. Always study your work. Don't wear jeans and T-shirt again when you visit me, they keep you too hot.' Then a new story confirms her respectability.

'The last funeral that I attended I told the pastor that I did not like the kind of dresses that the women were wearing in church. The amount of flesh showing is disrespectful in the Lord's House. I also told him "You are the shepherd, they are the flock. You should tell them your requirements." I surprised him when I said that, so he asked me: "Who are you?". I told him, "I am a woman and that is all you need to know."'

I bring the talk round to her earlier life and she tells me a story that I had not heard before.

'When I was a girl I used to go to mountain [*sic*] on my donkey to plant ground provisions. One day a man followed me and he tried to interfere with me. I had a cutlass and pushed it in his nose and turned it. He won't do that again. When I came to Kingstown I taught in my aunt's primary school. Some bright children passed through that school. They come to look for me now and then.' She mentions an eminent Caribbean banker. Proudly tells me how, by chance, they met outside a government office and his excited shout of her name and his eager embrace. She reminds me of how she did clerical work in my father's office. 'When it closed I managed the home-based sewing across the island. All of that put this roof over my head.'

'This roof' – a sturdy, unpainted concrete bungalow covered in galvanise and partly enclosed by an 'L'-shaped veranda – is one of the better-maintained houses on the bay front. There is a yard at the back with room for a flourishing mango tree. The town centre got a deepwater harbour, government buildings and a bus station. Shirley got a paved road in front of her house, and beyond that, rows of fishermen's shacks where they keep nets, boats, engines, boat parts. She no longer notices the obstructed view, but she warns the occupants: 'If the weather is rough you have to move. In the past the sea has reached my door.' Unlike many a Caribbean home, now usually enclosed in burglar-proof bars, her veranda is open and unfettered. Despite the area's tough reputation, security is not a problem for her. The district has its hierarchy and she is near the top, a sort of queen of Bottom Town.

She has long been a local Justice of the Peace. A passionate political party activist, she was appointed when the 'Son' Mitchell-led New Democratic Party (now in opposition and led by Arnhem Eustace) was in power. The incoming Government, her political opponents, tried to take the post from her, but failed. She used to be fetched at all hours in the night to witness statements given to the police, or if someone local was to be charged, but today she no longer goes to the police station after six in the evening. She tells me that the boys from the neighbourhood always ask for her if they are picked up. She says that her presence reassures them that they will not be unfairly treated or beaten up.

In many ways this scene is far from that of a conventional frontier situation, which is predominantly masculine and patriarchal. Instead, I have described a woman who has risen to a position of power in an area informally demarcated as a violent Kingstown location. Shirley's authority has partly grown out of party political activism, but her concern with decorum, standards and especially respectful dress also suggests her commitment to respectability. These represent very unfrontier-like traits, yet important frontier elements remain, not least the area's association with violence. In this context, Shirley is respected for her public service and her accomplishments, but her prestige depends on the useful skills she deploys, both as a Justice of the Peace to defend wayward youth, and working with what law exists in the neighbourhood to establish people's rights. Still, it's plain that the frontier is the site of a battle between urban order and its opposite, disorder. I see Shirley as one who has challenged the social boundaries in her earlier role of teacher, helping some of her past pupils across class barriers to become big-shots. But not so big that they ignore her influence.

To reassure me that I am safe under her roof while capturing, unconsciously, the common frontier nature of the area, she recounts the following story.

> One morning recently I notice a man not from here walk in front of my house. He passed a number of times and it made me curious, then suspicious. I thought it was odd. Khaki-shirt, who just cursed me off before you arrived, was nearby and also saw the man. He asked what the man wanted. Khaki-shirt did not trust what he heard. He told the man if he dared to touch me he would be dead.

She remains, then, important enough to be offered protection in her neighbourhood, a protection that she has in turn offered and continues to offer to unattached youth and those in need. The visit ends; we embrace. I step back over her little gate.

Figures on the front line 2: sketch of a frontiersman

Same island, different scene, yet linked to the previous one in significant ways. It is the 1950s, and in a large, secluded house on a cliff overlooking the turbulent meeting point and boundary clash of the Atlantic and the Caribbean, whose combined waves incessantly rush inshore to shatter on the rocks below, a small boy lives with his family.

When thunder-claps wake him at night and the sheet-lightning lights up his bedroom, without hesitation he races from his bed and crawls to safety between father and mother. Like many middle-class

West Indian children, he is indulged. He loves comic books – the large, brightly coloured American ones, and later the smaller, grittier black-and-white ones with British Second World War stories. This passion is one of the few he and his father share, and so the man funds and shares his son's insatiable appetite for them.

I cannot say that I knew my father well. Perhaps he did not want to be known. What I remember of his characteristics could fit on a postage stamp, but there were identifiable tendencies that were almost arche-typal. One style was *el hombre*, a hard-drinking rogue who loved to gamble – roulette, dog racing, cards – and could hold his liquor. He was a minor colony's Papa Hemingway with experience in Santo Domingo, where he had travelled in his early twenties, along with three or four friends, to work for Shell Oil. The details of what transpired there are little known, except that he learned to speak Spanish and prospered, returning as 'a person of means', eligible for marriage and a retail part-nership. Accordingly, he married my mother. White in appearance and educated in England, she met all the requirements of a 'good catch'. Their social life consisted of a few close friends and family, who would meet two or three times a week in each other's houses where the whisky flowed. At the height of these close gatherings Spanish would some-times spatter his conversation, a reminder of that other life. Like his father before him, he entered the retail business, though unlike him he succeeded in making his family financially secure.

My father attended school only up to the age of fifteen, but he valued education highly. By the time I was eight or nine years old, schooling was already competitive. A vague kind of character formation was aspired to on my behalf. The benchmark here was my cousin, my closest compan-ion, almost a brother. We were of similar age and attended the same government school, but he was 'bright' and invariably attained better marks than I did. Too wide a gap in our marks usually resulted in a dis-cussion about returning to the dame school that I have described earlier. That school aimed to instil the three 'R's in its pupils, which, apparently, the larger government school was incapable of doing to the satisfaction of my parents. And so a steady eye was kept on some fifteen of us as we parsed sentences, sweated through long division and compound inter-est calculations, practised our cursive style in large blue copy-books, and acquired a detailed knowledge of the King James Bible. The teacher, Miss John, was no slouch when it came to corporal punishment.

From his days in Santo Domingo, my father kept an ugly, snub-nosed .38 revolver locked in a polished wooden case in a tall bedroom ward-robe. On Sunday mornings the gun would occasionally be brought out for pistol practice. My mother would attend her high Anglican church devotions and he would blast away at rocks or old tin cans on the stony beach below our house. This noise was intended also to be a warning to anyone straying onto his land. Government misdeeds brought rough talk about 'people deserving to be shot'.

Sunday afternoons, when my homework – simple or compound interest calculations – was presented for my father's examination, were tinged with a vague fear of corporal punishment. A tortoise-shell-rimmed gaze made his enlarged eyes slightly forbidding. He had his own acute sense of right and wrong and did not entertain shades of grey. 'Churchill should have kept on fighting to roll back the Ruskies.' All politicians were 'scamps and thieves'. The uncertainty of change was anathema as political independence loomed. The island and the entire region were 'going to the dogs'. The curtain was descending on civilisa-tion as he knew it. All of this *hombre*-ness made the household wary in his presence. My mother used this to advantage, as she was the person through whom requests for outings and other events were invariably directed. If she did not approve of the request we were told to 'ask your father' and it ended there.

For a while he enjoyed playing golf. By the 1950s he was wealthy enough to buy a disused estate on the southernmost peninsula of the island that had been a course of nine holes in the late 1930s. He decided to revive it, making the club house on the cliff into the family home where I grew up. In a few years this dream of the sporting life collapsed. In the last twenty-five years or so of his life he showed little interest in physical exercise, preferring the routine of a few close friends and Scotch whisky.

The old-fashioned word 'merchant' suited him. His business part-nership thrived for some years while various other ventures came and went. When he and his siblings inherited parcels of land he became the informal family estate agent. His interest in landownership and sales increased as my mother independently inherited land from her family. Thus he managed the sale of real estate on her behalf as well as having an interest in a nearby arrowroot factory. In his latter years, he managed an insurance agency from a small office in the centre of Kingstown. So by the end of his life, this frontier product of a minor West Indian colony had been an overseas adventurer; local businessman; factory-owner; informal real estate agent and insurance manager; and, in island terms, had prospered in all capacities.

These two, Shirley Lynch and my father, each in their own way epit-omise frontier spirit, battling to uphold different kinds of respectabil-ity – he emphasising the individual, business-based ideas of legitimacy and civilisation while keeping the wild at bay by practising with his .38 revolver, she with her communally based ideas of respectability and civilisation. Perhaps it was inevitable their paths would cross, the wealthy businessman and the aspiring working-class woman. Each had something the other needed to prosper, and in its mutual dependency, it offered a not uncommon frontier relationship.

Epilogue

It's just nature, we say
this tsunami of empire that washed us up here.
   Final offer gentlemen. Five pounds three shillings
   for the seasoned buck.
When that last wave rolled back it exposed a humble butter fish
twitching, flipping and flapping, worn down town

   Five dollars for that heap?
   Ground provisions no longer cheap.
its mouth opening and closing

   You'd be amazed what deals can
   can be struck with care in our capital's
   little market square.

sucking its death of sea air wondering why its fins
fail to glide through water while its scales
slap the keel of some hard-hulled fishing boat.

> *Only thirty dollar Mother Lynch. Ah beg yuh,*
> *Mammy going send money for the wear and tear.*

When did we begin to ignore the hucksters
with their tight grip on the sidewalks

> *DRIVER! Why you can't look*
> *where you coming?*

their five shoe boxes, twenty-three pink plastic combs and
white trestle tables that groan with out-size brassieres?

> *RASTA! Why YOU can't go where you*
> *looking?*

We're cool with the pool of smart boys skulking in Middle Street
each with his three card stool waiting to fool the next passer-by

> *You and you family .... think they big-shot.*

while Sam solicits donations for his phantom football teams.

> *It have a funeral at four o'clock sharp.*

Who turns a hair when Bazodie marches through Market Square
wearing buttoned down wrists, short pants, head in a balaclava?

> *I wonder why people always have to die 'pon a*
> *week-day.*

With his termite ridden piece of treated pine he executes a perfect off
drive
and follows it through okras and eddoes in the firm belief that he is
Brian Lara.

> *He? He say he going to come back.*

And we look away when the rain fills the drains

> *Who want to go to Hell can go to Hell.*

and cockroaches thick as locusts swim out of the open gutters
like recently hatched leather-backs lost on their way to sea.

> *You are the shepherd, they are the flock*

But all's not lost. The wharf sign welcomes everyone
to a capital city proclaiming itself a 'hive of industry'

> *Boy, don't wear jeans and tee shirt again*
> *when you come to see me*
> *they keep you too hot.*
>
>   (Nanton, 2013–2014)

Notes

1 Total mainland population for 2007 was 92,110 (SVG, 2012: 12).

2 Thomas Webster Clarke, school inspector, in a police report of 1905 (quoted in Fraser, 2011: xx).

3 Boa cites one Methodist minister, the Revd Hudson, who, in 1849, described the tension created by these rebellious church members. From his statement it is apparent that the Shaker practices were viewed as distinct and unacceptable. Hudson reported to his General Secretaries: 'they insisted in holding meetings independent of and separate from our own, in which they indulged in the wildest enthusiasms and anathematising all who would not join in their excesses; indeed from the first we clearly saw that an "imperium in imperio" would never do and it is much to be regretted that our predecessors allowed such an organisation within our societies when at first by the expulsion of the ringleaders it might have been arrested, but being allowed to proceed with impunity they became more insolent and determined and led many astray' (Boa, 1998: 192).

4 Edward Cox identified among the leadership between the years 1900 and 1934 that some twenty-four were labourers, one a small proprietor, one a woodcutter; eleven other leaders had no identifiable occupation (Cox, 1993: 14).

5 Patricia Stephens describes the pattern of these links as 'a broken continuum, one which relied on ancestral memory, something disjointed … a wound which could be healed by shaping the Faith around the struggle for dignity in the hostile environment of the slaves' new world' (Stephens, 1999: 20).

6 Fraser notes that it was the magistrates who were given the final say to determine what was Shakerism. Actions that were used to determine the practice included 'binding of the head with white cloth, holding of lighted candles in hands, ringing a bell at intervals in meetings, violent shaking of body and limbs, shouting and grunting, flowers held in the hands of persons present and white chalk marks on the floor' (2001: 81).

7 Recent census figures indicate that except for the Pentecostal sect all other membership of religious denominations in SVG either declined rapidly or stagnated. In 2012 Spiritual Baptists held 8.9 per cent of total church membership.

8 This concern, Bonham Richardson argues, dominated official questions about control and direction (Richardson, 1997: 220).

9 One of the arguments presented by St Vincent planters against abolition was that freedom would result in slaves falling into habits of idleness and vice. That this belief continued is reflected in Hely-Hutchinson's concern.

10 Lyndon John estimates that the island's State-owned forest cover declined from 56 per cent in 1945 to 37 per cent by 1993. By 1995 it had shrunk again to 28.2 per cent (11,000 ha) and by 2000 had further declined to 15.4 per cent (6,000 ha) (John, 2006: 12–13).

11 The 2002 CANARI Technical Report outlining the integrated forestry strategy states that 'Significant portions of the state-owned forests were also turned into banana fields, either through illegal squatting, or with

the informal blessing of politicians who encouraged or allowed people to use portions of state property' (Cottle *et al.*, 2002: 2). Informal warnings prior to the 1998 'Weedeater' and the 2009 Vincy Pack ganja eradication raids were provided. Although there was considerable crop destruction, and some deaths resulted from the raids, some of the force of the raids was mitigated. Cottle suggests that the 'Weedeater' raid contributed to the overthrow of the Mitchell Government in 2001. He suggests also that ganja growers contributed to the popular sanction against the constitutional changes proposed by the Gonsalves-led Government in its second term of office between 2005 and 2009 (Cottle, 2010).

12 See Mike Kirkwood's foreword to this book.

13 In December 2014, it was reported in the *Stabroek News* that another pioneer, Conley 'Chivango' Rose, the coordinator of the National Marijuana Industry Association of SVG, is working to get a medical marijuana institute built in St Vincent because of the island's role as the leading cultivator in the eastern Caribbean. See Edmonds (2015).

7

Conclusion by way of afterword

I suspect that most gatekeepers have an intense dislike for frontiers, if not necessarily their role on the frontier. Their priority is to keep out the unwanted 'Other', and they are the first line of defence, internally, to keep things in order. Frontiers are unsettling, not least because of those individuals or groups who trouble them. This may account for the preference for looking towards modernity and 'civilisation', and the avoidance of the wild and wilderness. This unwillingness to look, however, does not mean that the wild has gone away. This work has suggested that, like those old perennials – taxation and death – the wild has remained very much with us in the Caribbean. This text has identified various kinds of 'boundary troublers' or 'boundary objects' at both the individual and the collective levels.[1] I am thinking here of the St Vincent ganja growers, the isolated surgeon, ganja bar owner, schoolteacher and woodsman.[2] I have suggested also that the 'wild' has found a way to reinvent itself, most recently by seeking protection in the form of TCMP in the Grenadines. So it appears that the 'wild' and 'civilised' relationship that I have navigated through these pages has been around for some time and is likely to be around for some time further. The question, then, is what is the value of reinterpreting the Caribbean through the lens of frontier? What might it offer in helping to understand SVG and the Caribbean region in relation to the world?

There are in principle two long-established alternative ways of looking at the world. One is to look for differences and the other is to search for common ground. Theorists of the Caribbean have for the most part made a plea for regional specificity and distinctiveness. I have in mind the early observations of Las Casas and his identification of the specificity of the region's way of dancing, Benitez-Rojo's observation of the Caribbean's syncopated way of walking, Lloyd Best's discussion of the specificity of Caribbean plantation society and culture, Kamau Brathwaite's historically based discussion of the Caribbean as the creole society par excellence, and Colin Wilson's teasing out the twin influences of 'reputation' and 'respectability' in Providentiales. These eminent thinkers about the Caribbean have unearthed identifiable and distinct trends that run through the region's culture.

Frontier analysis, on the other hand, falls within the perspective that searches for common ground. One of the uses of frontier analysis is, for example, in overcoming the intellectual impasse that has developed in the interdisciplinary field of 'island studies'. Lisa Fletcher has identified how this field has been undermined by an untheorised distinction between the relative values of 'geography' and 'literature'; island studies, she suggests, lacks a 'meta-discourse' about its scope and objects. She detects among island scholars a world view that suggests studying the real world is more meaningful than studying the imagined world. She states boldly: 'I am convinced that much of the anxiety I detect in debates about the best way to think and write about islands stems from an underlying distrust of literature' (Fletcher, 2011: 23). Certainly in the Caribbean there is limited crossover between those who study the 'hard' behavioural sciences and those in humanities. As Fletcher points out, this divide impedes interdisciplinary research and inhibits dialogue with related fields, for example postcolonial studies.

Beyond the boundary observed by Fletcher, frontier analysis is one way to circumvent this problem. Essentially it challenges the conventional boundaries within Caribbean humanities study at a fundamental level – those demarcating the sacrosanct disciplinary territories of literature and the so-called postcolonial canon, cultural studies, politics, history and so on. Such an analysis also extends well beyond the now somewhat tired cultural and nationalist island paradigm. The aim is not merely to critique from within, say, the world of Caribbean literary studies as it has traditionally been practised, as does a recent collection that – in critiquing the privileging of a specific group of postwar male writers, the ignoring of prewar writing, the marginalisation of writing by women, the prioritization of the 'folk' and the exclusion of the middle class and LGBT voices – extends rather than troubles the boundaries around canon formation.[3] It leaves untouched the question of literary boundaries between the official and unofficial, with regard, for example, to the status of popular fiction: 'The choice to be "popular" and therefore remain 'outside' rather than belonging to the circle of the elite is always partly an ideological one, an identification *otherwise* than with formal culture. Outsider fiction is a harbinger of change in Caribbean writing' (Bryce, 2014: 162). Early signs of this change began with Victor Headley's *Yardie*[4] and were manifested more recently in Marlon James's *A Brief History of Seven Killings*, which consciously challenges conventional notions of 'postcolonial' writing, and introduces all kinds of boundary crossing.[5] The winning of the 2015 Man Booker Prize by James for this novel might suggest canonisation, but if so, what canon? James's achievement transcends the boundary of Caribbean writing. The fact that it has been taken up by HBO to be made into a TV series arguably suggests its contiguity with other popular forms. Among his influences James cites William Faulkner, Roberto Bolano and comic books. 'A lot of what shaped my literary sensibilities were things like comics … The sort of cheap pulp fiction' (Farley, 2016). The novel is described by James as: 'Post-post-colonial', signifying 'a new generation of, well, new-ish generation of writers, where we're not driven by our dialogue with the former mother country. The hovering power for us when growing up in the '70s and '80s was not the UK. It was the States, it was America. And it wasn't an imperialistic power, it was just a cultural influence' (Mayer, 2015). My use of frontier theory, by significantly altering and enlarging the frame of analysis to take account of such 'cultural influences', enables a clearer understanding of the process to which James lays claim.

I should admit directly that in the chapters above I have become a sort of boundary troubler myself. For example, in Chapters 5 and 6

I specifically offer a frontier analysis that brings together different genres of writing, namely historical travel writing, politics, the novel, monologue, poetry and autobiography. This approach incorporates both the 'real' and 'invented' worlds of one island's political imaginary, opening up the scope of analysis rather than closing it down. It says, indirectly, and thus politely: to hell with any canon – if the frontier frame in use can bear it, why can't the writing of a nineteenth-century colonial magistrate be compared and contrasted with that of a living female Canadian canonical author, or a political novel with two hack political autobiographies? A frontier analysis thus both opens up the range of possible objects for examination and changes the frame, enabling a process of compare-and-contrast that extends beyond the insular and restricted geography of regional writing.

Frontier analysis starts from the common ground that the region shares with the rest of the world – notions of 'boundaries', 'civilisation' and 'wilderness', however defined. Awareness of the way these notions are applied enables a dialogue, not only among individual island states in the Caribbean, but with anywhere else globally that has a frontier, and thus affords the opportunity to participate more fully in the worldwide debate on globalisation – one that defines our times and will continue to do so for the foreseeable future. A frontier perspective that alters and enlarges the frame of analysis to include history, literature and culture extends the ground of the debate and increases the visibility of otherwise relatively insignificant island states. Speaking across boundaries, the Caribbean emerges as a powerful metaphor of globalisation itself. As my friend said in the preface, we roar.

Notes

1 The phrases are Kavita Philip's. She notes that 'tracking boundary objects helps us trace anxieties about the fields coalescing around them … [they] trouble civilized discourses around the notion of government, always assumed to be on the side of the modern' (Philip, 2014: 165).

2 These frontierspeople, for the most part, are nearer to Odysseus than to Achilles. As explained by Adam Nicholson, 'These are the two possibilities for human life. You can either do what your integrity tells you to do, or

niftily find your way around the obstacles life throws in your path ... Which will you be? Achilles or Odysseus, the monument of obstinacy and pride or the slippery trickster in whom nothing is certain and from whom nothing can be trusted? The singular hero or the ingenious man?' (Nicholson, 2014: 60).

3 See Brown and Rosenburg (2015), 3–24.
4 For an analysis of the influence of this novel and the publishing storm it brought in its wake see Farred (2002).
5 See my review of *A Brief History of Seven Killings* (Nanton, 2015).

References

Archer, A. J., 1932, *Guide Book to St Vincent*, 7th edn, revised, Kingstown: n.p.

Atwood, Margaret, 1998 [1981], *Bodily Harm*, New York: Penguin.

Austin-Broos, D., 1996, 'Politics and the Redeemer: State and Religion as Ways of Being in Jamaica', *New West Indian Guide*, 70.1–2: 59–90.

Barich, Bill, 1997, 'The Victim's Wake', *Outside Magazine*, November, http://www.outsideonline.com/1833201/victims-wake (accessed 18 July 2016).

Bayley, Frederick William Naylor, 1833, *Four Years' Residence in the West Indies during the Years 1826, 7, 8, and 9, by a Son of a Military Officer*, London: William Kidd.

Benitez-Rojo, 1996 [1992], *Repeating Island: The Caribbean and the Postmodern Perspective*, trans. James Maraniss, 2nd edn, Durham, NC and London: Duke University Press.

Boa, Sheena, 1998, 'Colour, Class and Gender in Post-Emancipation St Vincent 1834–1884', unpublished PhD thesis, University of Warwick.

Boa, Sheena, 2002, 'Setting the Law in Defiance: Urban Protests and Lieutenant Governor Edward John Eyre in Post Emancipation St Vincent 1838–1861', *Caribbean Studies*, 30.2: 130–148.

Bongie, Chris, 1995, 'The Last Frontier: Memories of the Postcolonial Future in Keri Hulme's *The Bone People*', in Rob Wilson and Arif Dirlik (eds), *Asia/Pacific as a Space of Cultural Production*, Durham, NC and London: Duke University Press, 226–49.

Bongie, Chris, 1998, *Islands and Exiles: The Creole Identities of Post/Colonial Literature*, Stanford: Stanford University Press.

Boyce, Rubert W., 1910, *Health Progress and Administration in the West Indies*, London: J. Murray.

Brown, A. and C. Stone, 1976, *Essays on Power and Change in Jamaica*, Kingston: Kingston Publishers.

Brown, Dillon J. and Leah Reade Rosenburg (eds), 2015, 'Introduction: Looking beyond Windrush', in *Beyond Windrush: Rethinking Postwar Anglophone Caribbean Literature*, Jackson: University Press of Mississippi, 3–24.

Brown, Stewart and Mark McWatt (eds), 2005, *The Oxford Book of Caribbean Verse*, Oxford: Oxford University Press.

Bryce, Jane, 2014, 'Adventures in Form: "Outsider" Fiction in the Caribbean', in Andrew O. Lindsay (ed.), *Beacons of Excellence: The Edgar Mittelholzer*

Memorial Lectures, 3 vols, Vol. I: 1967–2014, [Georgetown]: Caribbean Press, 145–163.

Carmichael, A. C., 1834, *Domestic Manners and Social Conditions of the White, Coloured, and Negro Population of the West Indies,* 2 vols, London: Whittaker, Treacher.

Chevannes, Barry, 1971, 'Revival and the Black Struggle', *Savacou: Journal of the Caribbean Artists Movement,* 5: 27.

Chevannes, Barry, 1999, '*Coming in from the Cold: Native Religions and the Problem of Democracy in Jamaica*', in Yamada Mitsuo and Carlos Ivan Degregori (eds), *Estados nacionales, etnicidad y democracia en América Latina,* Osaka: Japan Centre for Area Studies, [n.p.].

Child, Vivian M., 2004, *City of Arches: Memories of an Island Capital, Kingstown, St Vincent and the Grenadines,* Toronto: Cybercom.

Cottle, Junior, 'Spirit', 2010, 'The Politics of Marijuana in St Vincent and the Grenadines', *Agencia prensa rural,* http://prensarural.org/spip/spip.php?article4799 (accessed 15 April 2016).

Cottle, Junior, Stephen Koestler, FitzGerald Providence and Yves Renard, 2002, 'Developing an Integrated Forest Management and Rural Livelihoods Project in St Vincent and the Grenadines: A Case Study', CANARI Technical Report no. 326, European Commission.

Cox, Edward L., 1993, 'Religious Intolerance and Persecution: The Case of the Shakers of St Vincent, 1900–1934', paper presented at the 18th Annual Conference of the Caribbean Studies Association, 24–29 May 1993, http://ufdcimages.uflib.ufl.edu/CA/00/40/01/21/00001/PDF.pdf (accessed 15 April 2016).

Cyrus, Cecil, 1989, *A Clinical and Pathological Atlas: The Records of a Surgeon in St Vincent, the West Indies,* Montrose: A. Cecil Cyrus.

Curtin, Philip D., 1990, *The Rise and Fall of the Planter Complex: Essays in Atlantic History,* Cambridge: Cambridge University Press.

Das, Veena and Deborah Poole (eds), 2004, *Anthropology in the Margins of the State,* Santa Fe and Oxford: James Curry.

Drayton, Richard, 2000, *Nature's Government: Science, Imperial Britain, and the 'Improvement' of the World,* New Haven and London: Yale University Press.

Drayton, Richard, 2004, 'The Problem of the Hero(ine) in Caribbean History', Elsa Goveia Lecture, University of the West Indies, Cave Hill, Barbados.

Edmonds, Kevin, 2015, 'Ganja and Globalization in St Vincent', *Stabroek News,* www.stabroeknews.com (accessed 26 May 2015).

Fabel, Robin F. A., 2000, *Colonial Challenges: Britons, Native Americans, and Caribs: 1759–1775*, Gainesville, University Press of Florida.

Farley, Christopher John, 2016, 'Writer Marlon James Reimagines a Watershed in Jamaica', *Wall Street Journal*, 2 October 2014, www.wsj.com (accessed 23 January 2016).

Farred, Grant, 2002, 'The Postcolonial Chickens Come Home to Roost: How *Yardie* Has Created a New Postcolonial Subaltern', *South Atlantic Quarterly*, 100.1: 287–305.

Fineman, Mark, 2000, 'Seeds of Distress in St Vincent', *The Baltimore Sun*, 28 January, http://articles.baltimoresun.com/2000-01-28/news/0001280218_1_marijuana-vincent-island-economy (accessed 2 August 2016).

Fletcher, Lisa, 2011, '" … some distance to go': A Critical Survey of Island Studies', *New Literatures Review*, Islands Special, 23: 17–34.

Fraser, Adrian, 2002, *Chatoyer (Chatawae), the First National Hero of St Vincent and the Grenadines*, St Vincent: Galaxy.

Fraser, Adrian, 2011, *From Shakers to Spiritual Baptists: The Struggle for Survival of the Shakers of St Vincent and the Grenadines*, St Vincent and the Grenadines: Kings SVG.

Gonsalves, Ralph E., 2001, *The Politics of Our Caribbean Civilisation: Essays and Speeches*, Kingstown: Great Works Depot.

Gonsalves, Ralph E., 2010a, *Diary of a Prime Minister: Ten Days among Benedictine Monks*, St Vincent and the Grenadines: SFI Books.

Gonsalves, Ralph E., 2010b, *The Making of 'The Comrade': The Political Journey of Ralph Gonsalves: An Autobiographical Sketch of a Caribbean Prime Minister*, St Vincent and the Grenadines: Strategy Forum.

Grosfoguel, R., 1995, 'Colonial Caribbean Migrations to the Metropolis in Comparative Perspective', paper presented at the 'Comparative History of Migration within the Caribbean and Europe' conference, Oxford Brooks University, Oxford.

Hall, C. Michael, 2002, 'The Changing Cultural Geography of the Frontier: National Parks and Wilderness as Frontier Remnant', in Shaul Krakover and Yehua Gradus (eds), *Tourism in Frontier Areas*, Oxford: Lexington Books.

Harris, Wilson, 1981, 'The Frontier on which *Heart of Darkness* Stands', *Research in African Literatures*, 12.1: 86–93.

Henke, H. and D. D. Marshall, 2003, 'The Legitimacy of Neo-Liberal Trade Regimes in the Caribbean: Issues of "Race", Class and Gender', in C. Barrow-Giles and D. Marshall (eds), *Living at the Borderlines: Issues in Caribbean Sovereignty and Development*, Kingston: Ian Randle.

Hennessy, Alistair, 1978, *The Frontier in Latin American History*, London: Edward Arnold.

Higman, Barry W., 1984, *Slave Populations of the British Caribbean 1807–1834*, Mona: University of the West Indies Press.

International Maritime Organization, 2004, *Reports on Acts of Piracy and Armed Robbery against Ships*, fourth quarterly report (October–December 2003), London: International Maritime Organization.

Jacobs, Curtis, 2003, *The Brigands' War in St Vincent: The View from the French Records, 1794–1796*, St Vincent Country Conference Re-prints, University of the West Indies, Cave Hill, http://www.uwichill.edu.bb/bnccde/svg/conference/papers/filename.html (accessed 16 July 2016).

James, Marlon, 2014, *A Brief History of Seven Killings*, New York: Riverhead Books.

John, Lyndon, 2006, 'From Growing Ganja to Planting Trees: Stimulating Legal Livelihoods and Watershed Management in St Vincent through Payments from Public Utilities', Who Pays for Water?, Project Document no. 2, Laventille: CANARI.

John, Rupert, 2009 [1979], *Pioneers in Nation-Building in a Caribbean Mini-State*, St Vincent: Kings SVG.

Johnson, Erika, 2013, 'Gangs Are the New Law in Urban Trinidad and Tobago', *Sight Crime*, 21 October 2013.

Kairi Consultants Ltd, 2008, *St Vincent and the Grenadines Country Poverty Assessment, 2007/2008*, Vol. I: *Living Conditions in a Caribbean Small Island Developing State*', Port-of-Spain, Kairi Consultants Ltd.

King, Baldwin and Cheryl Phills King (eds), 2011, *Caribbean Trailblazers*, 2 vols, Madison: Kings SVG.

Kirby, I. E. and C. I. Martin, 1986, *The Rise and Fall of the Black Caribs*, 2nd edn, Kingstown: [n.p.].

Klein, Axel, 2004, 'The Ganja Industry and Alternative Development in St Vincent and the Grenadines', in Axel Klein, Marcus Day and Anthony Harriott (eds), Caribbean Drugs: From Criminalization to Harm Reduction, London: Zed Books, 224–244.

Legair, I. N., [n.d.], 'Asset Protection: How to Protect Your Assets from Greedy Spouses and Inconsiderate Creditors', http://www.stvincentoffshore.net/how-to-protect-your-assets-from-greedy-spouses-and-inconsiderate-creditors/ (accessed 21 May 2015).

Leigh-Fermor, Patrick, 2005 [1950], *The Traveller's Tree: A Journey through the Caribbean Islands*, London: John Murray.

Lemar, Howard Roberts and Leonard Monteath Thompson (eds), 1981, *The Frontier in History: North America and Southern Africa Compared*, New Haven and London: Yale University Press.

Levy, Claude, 1980, *Emancipation, Sugar and Federalism: Barbados and the West Indies 1822–1876*, Gainsville: University Presses of Florida.

Lewis, Gordon, K., 1968, *The Growth of the Modern West Indies*, London: MacGibbon and Kee.

Lewis, Gordon K., 1983, *Main Currents in Caribbean Thought: The Historical Evolution of Caribbean Society in Its Ideological Aspects 1492–1900*, Baltimore and London: Johns Hopkins University Press.

Lewis, Linden, 2003, *Exploring the Intersections of Gender, Sexuality and Culture in the Caribbean*, Gainsville: University of Florida Press.

Lewis, Paul E., 2010, 'Would Canouan Development Resorts Limited Chart a New Path?', *Caribbean News Now*, 30 November 2010, http://www carib-beannewsnow.com (accessed 17 July 2016).

Lowe, H. I. L., 1972, 'Jamaican Folk Medicine', *Jamaica Journal*, 6.2: 20–24.

McDonald, Roderick A., 1996, 'Urban Crime and Social Control in St Vincent during the Apprenticeship', in Roderick A. McDonald (ed.), *West Indies Accounts: Essays he History of the British Caribbean and the Atlantic Economy in Honor of Richard Sheridan*, Kingston: Press University of the West Indies.

McDonald, Roderick A. (ed.), 2001, *Between Slavery and Freedom: Special Magistrate John Anderson's Journal of St Vincent during Apprenticeship*, Barbados: University of the West Indies Press.

Marshall, Woodville K., 1981, ' "Vox Populi": The St Vincent Riots and Disturbances of 1862', Seminar Paper no.2, University of the West Indies, Cave Hill, Barbados.

Marshall, Woodville and Bridget Brereton, 1999, 'Historiography of Barbados, the Windward Islands, Trinidad and Tobago and Guyana', in *General History of the Caribbean, 6 vols, Vol. VI: Methodology and Historiography of the Caribbean*, ed. Barry W. Higman, London and Oxford: UNESCO and Macmillan Caribbean, 544–603.

Martin, Robert Montgomery, 1837, *History of the West Indies Comprising British Guyana, Barbados, St Vincent's, St Lucia, Dominica, Montserrat, Antigua, St Christopher's etc.*, British Colonial Library 5, London: Whittaker and Co.

Martin, Robert Montgomery, 1843, *History of the Colonies of the British Empire in the West Indies, South America, North America, Asia, Austral-Asia, Africa and Europe*, Official Records of the Colonial Office, London: Dawson's of Pall Mall.

Mayer, Petra, 2015, 'Marlon James Wins Man Booker Prize', http://www.npr. org/sections/thetwo-way/2015/10/13/448397179/marlon-james-wins-man-booker-prize (accessed 23 January 2016).

Meyerhoff, Miriam and James A. Walker, 2013, *Bequia Talk (St Vincent and the Grenadines)*, Colombo and London: Battlebridge.

Mignolo, Walter D., 2000, *Local Histories/Global Designs: Coloniality, Subaltern Knowledges and Border Thinking*, Princeton: Princeton University Press.

Mill, John Stewart, 1968 [1848], *Principles of Political Economy*, London: Longman, Green and Dyer.

Mitchell, James F., 1989, *Caribbean Crusade*, Waitsfield: Concepts Publishing.

Mitchell, James F., 1996, *Guiding Change in the Islands*, Waitsfield: Concepts Publishing.

Mitchell, James F., 2006, *Beyond the Islands: An Autobiography*, Oxford: Macmillan Caribbean.

Naipaul, V. S., 1996, *The Middle Passage*, London: Pan Macmillan.

Nanton, Philip, 1983, 'The Changing Pattern of State Control in St Vincent and the Grenadines', in R. Cohen and F. Ambursley (eds), *Crisis in the Caribbean*, London: Heinemann, 223–246.

Nanton, Philip, 1984, 'Strategy and Tactics in Organisational Change, Race Relations and Local Government', *Local Government Studies*, 10.5: 51–60.

Nanton, Philip, 1992, 'I', in Stewart Brown and Ian McDonald (eds), *The Heinemann Book of Caribbean Poetry*, Oxford: Heinemann Educational Publishers, 165.

Nanton, Philip, 2004, 'Rethinking Privatization, the State and Illegal Drugs in the Commonwealth Caribbean', in Axel Klein, Marcus Day and Anthony Harriott (eds), *Caribbean Drugs: From Criminalization to Harm Reduction*, London and New York: Zed Books; Kingston: Ian Randle.

Nanton, Philip, 2006, 'At the Cyrus Museum, Beat Profile', *Caribbean Beat*, 78 (March/April): 52–55.

Nanton, Philip, 2013–2014, 'Flotsam and Jetsam', *BIM: Arts for the 21st Century*, 6: 41–43.

Nanton, Philip, 2014a, *Island Voices from St Christopher and the Barracudas*, London and Trafalgar, Dominica: Papillote Press.

Nanton, Philip, 2014b, 'Song of Chatoyee', in Georgie Horrell, Aisha Spencer and Morag Styles (eds), *Give the Ball to the Poet: A New Anthology of Caribbean Poetry*, London: Commonwealth Education Trust Books.

Nanton, Philip, 2015, review of *A Brief History of Seven Killings*, *Journal of West Indian Literature*, 23: 1–2.

Nanton, Philip with M. FitzGerald, 1990, 'Race Policies in Local Government: Boundaries or Thresholds?', in W. Ball and J. Solomos (eds), *Race and Local Politics*, London: Macmillan, 155–174.

Nash, Roderick Frazier, 2001, *Wilderness and the American Mind*, 4th edn, New Haven: Yale University Press.

Naylor, R. T., 2002, *Wages of Crime: Black Markets, Illegal Finance and the Underworld Economy*, Ithaca, NY: Cornell University Press.

Nicholson, Adam, 2014, *The Mighty Dead: Why Homer Matters*, London: William Collins.

Pares, Richard, 1960, *A West India Fortune*, London: Longman, Green.

Patterson, Orlando, 1967. *The Sociology of Slavery: An Analysis of the Origin, Development and Structure of Negro Slave Society in Jamaica*, London: MacGibbon and Kee.

Philip, Kavita, 2014, 'Keep on Copyin' in the Free World? Genealogies of the Postcolonial Pirate Figure,' in Lars Eckstein and Anja Schwarz (eds), *Postcolonial Piracy: Media Distribution and Cultural Production in the Global South*, London and New York: Bloomsbury, 149–178.

Pratt, M. L., 1992, *Imperial Eyes: Travel Writing and Transculturation*, London: Routledge.

Premdas, R. R., 2002, 'Self Determination and Sovereignty in the Caribbean: Migration, Transnational Identities and Deterritorialisation of the State', in Ramesh Ramsaran (ed.), *Caribbean Survival and the Global Challenge*, Kingston: Ian Randle, 47–63.

Reid, S., 1980, 'Economic Elites in Jamaica: A Study in Monistic Influence', *Anthropologica*, 22.1: 25–44.

Richardson, Bonham C., 1992, *The Caribbean in the Wider World 1499–1992*, Cambridge: Cambridge University Press.

Richardson, Bonham C., 1997, *Economy and Environment in the Caribbean: Barbados and the Windwards in the Late 1800s*, Mona: University of the West Indies Press.

Roudette, Vonnie, 2009, *The Nature of Belonging: Groundings in the Earth of Daily Life*, [n.p.]: Strategy Forum.

St Vincent and the Grenadines [SVG], 2012, 'Population and Vital Statistics Report', Kingstown: Statistical Office.

Schwartz, Mattathias, 2011, 'A Massacre in Jamaica', *The New Yorker*, 12 December 2011.

Segal, Aaron, 1996, 'Locating the Swallows: Caribbean Recycling Migration', paper presented to the Caribbean Studies Association Conference, San Juan, Puerto Rico, 27–31 May.

Sharman, J. C., 2011, *The Money Laundry: Regulating Criminal Finance in the Global Economy*, Ithaca, NY: Cornell University Press.

Shepherd, Charles, 1831, *An Historical Account of the Island of St Vincent*, London: Cass.

Singham, Archie, 1968, *The Hero and the Crowd in a Colonial Polity*, New Haven: Yale University Press.

Slotkin, Richard, 1973, *Regeneration through Violence: The Mythology of the American Frontier, 1600–1860*, Middletown, CT: Wesleyan University Press.

Smart, Samantha, 2001, letter to the Editor, *Searchlight*, 9 February, 11.

Spinelli, Joseph, 1973, 'Land Use and Population in St Vincent 1763–1960: A Contribution to the Study of Patterns of Economic and Demographic Change in a Small West Indian Island', Ph.D. thesis, University of Florida.

Spurr, David, 1993, *The Rhetoric of Empire: Colonial Discourse in Journalism, Travel Writing and Imperial Administration*, Durham, NC and London: Duke University Press.

Stephens, Patricia, 1999, *The Spiritual Baptist Faith: African New World Religious History, Identity and Testimony*, London: Karnak House.

Strachan, Ian Gregory, 2002, *Paradise and Plantation: Tourism and Culture in the Anglophone Caribbean*, Charlottesville and London: University of Virginia Press.

Thomas, G. C. H., 1989 [1972], *Ruler in Hiroona: A West Indian Novel*, London and Basingstoke: Macmillan.

Thomas-Hope, Elizabeth M., 1992, *Explanation in Caribbean Migration Perceptions of the Image: Jamaica, Barbados and St Vincent*, Warwick University Caribbean Studies, Oxford: Macmillan Caribbean.

Thorburn, M. J., 1974, 'Jamaican Bushes and Human Chromosomes', *Jamaica Journal*, 8.4: 18–19.

Tidrick, G., 1973, 'Some Aspects of Jamaican Emigration to the United Kingdom 1953–1962', in Lambros Comitas and David Lowenthal (eds), *Work and Family Life: West Indian Perspectives*, New York: Anchor Press/ Doubleday.

Trollope, Anthony, 1859, *The West Indies and the Spanish Main*, London: Chapman and Hall.

United Nations Office on Drugs and Crime [UNODC], 2003, 'Caribbean Drugs Trends 2001–2002', Bridgetown: Caribbean Regional Office.

United Nations Office on Drugs and Crime [UNODC], 2007, 'Crime, Violence and Development Trends: Costs and Policy Options in the Caribbean', Report no. 37820, http://www.unodc.org/pdf/research/Cr_and_Vio_Car_E.pdf (accessed 21 May 2015).

United Nations Office on Drugs and Crime [UNODC], 2012, 'Sexual Violence', http://www.unodc.org/documents/data-and-analysis/statistics/crime/CTS_Sexual_violence.xls (accessed 2 August 2016).

Van Lier, R. A. J., 1971 [1949], *Frontier Society: A Social Analysis of the History of Surinam*, trans. M. J. L. van Yperen, The Hague: Martinus Nijhoof.

Vaughn, Roger, 1994, *Mustique*, New York and Mustique: Arne Hasselqvist and Alfred Scheitzman.

Waters, Ivor, 1964, *The Unfortunate Valentine Morris*, Newport, Wales: R. H. Johns.

Weaver, Rebecca, 2007, *Empire Islands: Castaways, Cannibals and Fantasies of Conquest*, Minneapolis: University of Minnesota Press.

Wilkinson, Alec, 2009, 'Not Quite Cricket: Is a Billionaire Accused of Fraud Also Damaging a Noble Sport?', *New Yorker*, 9 March 2009, http://www.newyorker.com/magazine/2009/03/09/not-quite-cricket (accessed 17 July 2016).

Index

Lightning Source UK Ltd.
Milton Keynes UK
UKOW05f0202040217
293546UK00008B/220/P